HANDBOOK TO HAPPINESS

HANDBOOK
TO
HAPPINESS

CHARLES R. SOLOMON

Tyndale House
Publishers, Inc.
Wheaton, Illinois

To my wife, Sue, who has shared and suffered with me
as my life was shaped on God's anvil
that I might begin to be "conformed to his image" (Rom. 8:29).

All Scripture quotations are from the King James
Version of the Bible.

This book was originally published under the title
Handbook of Happiness by House of Solomon,
Denver, Colorado. The first edition was published by
Tyndale House Publishers by arrangement with
House of Solomon. The poems omitted from the re-
vised edition may be found in a book entitled *Hand-
book to Happiness in Verse,* which is published by
the author.

The material in this book may be used by laymen
and pastors in sharing with others how their deepest
needs may be met. It is not to be used in any professional counseling office or practice advertised as
Spirituotherapy except as duly authorized by Grace
Fellowship International, P.O. Box 27315, Denver,
CO 80227-0315. (303) 980-0003.

Library of Congress Catalog Card Number 88-51829
ISBN 0-8423-1283-8
Copyright 1971, 1989 by Charles R. Solomon
All rights reserved
Printed in the United States of America

99 98 97 96 95
12 11 10 9 8

CONTENTS

PREFACE

It has now been more than seventeen years since I wrote the first edition of this book. I believe it is time to update it and to add material that supplements and substantiates its message. Since I had been counseling for less than two years when I wrote the first edition, the lives impacted were fewer, and the influence of the ministry was limited to the state of Colorado.

The original first chapter, revised and updated, now appears at the end of the book, since some have stumbled over the psychological terminology and had given up on reading the book. Some have objected to my taking a firm stand relative to approaches to counseling that are not centered on the believer's relationship to the cross of Christ. Others have said that I was too lenient in exposing the degree to which secular thinking has influenced accepted norms in Christian psychology and psychiatry today.

I realize that mine is decidedly the minority opinion. Yet, it is a conviction given by God. And, as with Luther in the Reformation, I must stand true to the illumination I have received and let those who object sort out their convictions for themselves. Obviously, those who have opted for a more psychological approach, those who object to a theology that holds to the necessity of what we will in this book describe as "the exchanged life" and "the experienced cross" will never be a friend to this approach.

Over the years, God has called many others to share in the ministry, and literally thousands of lives have been touched by the Spirit of God in this and other countries. Some of those whose lives have been transformed had been defeated Christians. Some were lost and have found the Savior. Others had been afflicted with debilitating emotional disturbances, and many had difficulties with interpersonal relationships. Many of these would have been classified as severely neurotic and some had been labeled psychotic, though we do not use such labels in our dealing with people in the counseling situation.

Counseling and training centers have been established in several states and foreign countries. Grace Fellowship International (GFI) has directly established works in Indiana, Missouri, Georgia, and Florida in addition to the center in Denver, and a number of spin-off ministries have developed around the country that have been greatly used of God.

In addition to the ministries in this country, centers have been established in Argentina, India, Australia, Egypt, and Korea. Training in varying degrees has now been done on six continents. *Handbook to Happiness* has been published in Spanish and two editions in Korean. An English edition has also been published in India. Chapter two has been condensed into tract form for use in personal work, called *The Wheel and the Line* (available through GFI), which has been published in ten languages. Several other language editions are in process, the publication of which will make it possible to introduce the message and methods of Spirituotherapy into other strategic parts of the world.

In the beginning, the ministry was limited to counseling as a means of propagating the truth of freedom through union with Christ in his death and resurrection. It was necessary to prove to critics of this method that a viable integration of counseling and the Word of God done in the power of the Holy Spirit was sufficient to meet the deepest needs of man. Then it had to be proven that it was not a personality cult but that others from all walks of life and in various cultures and languages could be taught to apply the same approach to the resolution of life problems and see it honored by the Spirit of God.

This having been accomplished, GFI is now turning its attention to getting out the message of the cross through missionary endeavors in various parts of the world. The international offices presently established are having a significant impact, but there is a need for many more in this country who will go to strategic contacts in various countries to introduce this proven approach to communicating the truth of our identification with Christ. Much of this can be done by volunteers who can take a short-term mission trip to share with a believer, who already understands the message, how it can be communicated on a one-to-one basis. Those who are not able to go to a foreign country can work with us to extend the message of the cross to other communities and states.

The network of believers who have read the first edition of this book forms a pool from which to draw to send volunteer missionaries literally to the four corners of the earth. Pray with us that many will be challenged to become short-term volunteer missionaries to strengthen the Body of Christ in this country and around the world.

This book goes out with the prayer that many will see its message as appropriate, if not for their own needs, for many of their friends and families. Many have found victory. Some have even returned from the brink of suicide as the Holy Spirit used the simple presentation of our resources in Christ to meet them at their extremity. May he meet you at the point of your need in life and ministry.

INTRODUCTION

Spirituotherapy is a word coined by Dr. Solomon to identify an approach to counseling that makes the believer's relationship to the cross of Christ central to its method and goal. In Spirituotherapy, the Holy Spirit is the therapist who renews the mind and transforms the life in accord with Romans 12:2. Spirituotherapy was pioneered at Grace Fellowship International (GFI), incorporated in the state of Colorado in 1969 as a nonprofit corporation to implement a spiritual counseling ministry. It has been recognized by the Internal Revenue Service as a public foundation, a tax-exempt religious organization. GFI is nondenominational, and its allegiance is to the Lord Jesus Christ and to the infallible and immutable Word of God.

Dr. Solomon, founder and president of GFI, received his B.S. degree from East Tennessee State University and his Master of Personnel Service degree from the University of Colorado. Dr. Solomon began counseling part time while employed with Martin Marietta Corporation where he worked after completing undergraduate work in 1951 until 1970. This counseling was under a contract with the Department of Labor where Martin Marietta was to hire and train "hard-core unemployed" females for clerical work. His master's thesis was based on the results of that program.

He earned the Doctor of Education degree from the University of Northern Colorado. Much of the work toward this degree was in original research, counseling, writing, and teaching associated with the discipline of Spirituotherapy. The remainder was in counseling and psychology. The first edition of this book was his project in lieu of a doctoral dissertation.

The first GFI office opened on February 1, 1970 in Denver, Colorado. The first branch office was opened in 1975, and the first international office was opened in Argentina in January, 1981. Thousands of people from six continents and many countries have received some type of training, which began with the first seminar in Colorado Springs in 1972. In 1983, the Exchanged Life Foundation (ELF) was formed to act as a funding arm for extending the message of the cross. Contributions to the foundation, as gifts to Grace Fellowship International, are tax deductible.

Inquiries about the mission of GFI and contributions may be addressed to:

Grace Fellowship International
P.O. Box 27315
Denver, CO 80227

The poems that were originally published in the first edition may now be found, along with a number of others, in a new book entitled *Handbook to Happiness in Verse*. This book may be obtained at the above address or from the author.

ONE
EXPERIENCING THE
CROSS OF CHRIST

Knowing what the world is like today, it is certain that you or some of those you love are facing problems that are impossible to resolve or to face in the strength of human resources. A pastor I talked with recently said many pastors today are experiencing severe pressure in their ministries. He spoke of problems in the pastors' own lives, their families, and conflicts within the life of the church. He further stated that this was not true even ten years ago.

Loyalty to the local church seems to be at an all-time low, which is to be expected as a logical result of the breakdown of family structures. This, along with the usual problems faced by pastors, puts them in a rather unenviable position.

I understand what my pastor friend was talking about, because part of my past experience in dealing with just such pressure, I believe, has helped me find some answers. I believe an understanding of some of the concepts of rejection and identity is vital in dealing with these pressures. And though not everyone has the help of a counselor, we all have access to the infallible Word of God and *the Counselor*, the Holy Spirit who alone is able to transform our lives by the renewing of our minds, as the Apostle Paul promised in Romans 12:2.

I was one of those who did not have the opportunity to share my needs with another believer who could point me to the answer from the Scriptures, either for the meaning of salvation or for advice about the rest of my spiritual journey. Although I had trusted Christ as a seventeen-year-old, I entered the kingdom still carrying a load of emotional problems that hindered my effectiveness in facing normal activities, to say nothing of the stresses of life.

I grew up with more than my share of inferiority feelings along with an ability to hide these feelings from others. I enjoyed my school years as far as the academics were concerned but was uncomfortable socially. Even though I had somewhat better than average intelligence, I felt I would fail at the mundane pursuits of life. My high school years were very unhappy and I viewed graduation as an escape from an intolerable existence.

I was determined to get through college, even though I felt like I would flunk out. I studied fairly hard the first quarter and made straight A's and the dean's list. Even so, it did not change the way I *felt*. I *knew* I would find some way to make above average grades while *feeling* that everyone in the class knew more than I did. During my childhood, I had been programmed by circumstances for my mind to go one way and my emotions another.

In my second year of college, I met my wife and right away tried to convince her of how inferior I was. However, she saw my above average academic performance and found it difficult to believe that I was as inferior as I presented myself to be. We were married between my junior and senior years, and she taught school while I completed my last year. I had begun a preengineering major, since I found it unthinkable to consider a career that involved public speaking. Stage fright had severely limited my options. I finally wound up majoring in mathematics and getting a teaching credential, even though I didn't want to teach. Finally, I was hired by what is now Martin Marietta Corporation in Baltimore, Maryland, and set about to try behaving like an engineer. I felt inferior in the profession for which I had been prepared, so you can imagine how I felt in one for which I had little preparation.

Our three children were born by the time I was twenty-six.

This period, my twenties, was a time of inner conflict. I had severe depression and anxiety and an ulcer by the time I was twenty-five and was taking 400 mg. of Thorazine a day for a while during my mid-twenties. At the age of twenty-seven, I sold out completely to the Lord Jesus Christ but did not know where to go from there. I got involved in the church, working very hard, but found that working for the Lord didn't necessarily produce spiritual growth. I accepted a transfer with the corporation to Denver, where we became involved in a solid, Bible-believing church, and I continued the ceaseless rounds of compulsive service. My responsibilities increased in my employment and my family, but my capacity to produce was diminished by the increasing depression and anxiety. Obviously, my employment and continuous work for the church in my off hours took up most of the time I should have had for my family. This, along with the severe emotional problems, did little to commend me as a husband and father.

When I could get my mind off of myself and become involved in some kind of activity, I could enjoy myself to some degree. But the unresolved conflict was always just beneath the surface. At age thirty-four, I was tentatively diagnosed as having multiple sclerosis, which was never confirmed. I was privately disappointed that it was not cancer. Dying with cancer would have provided what I would have considered an honorable discharge from life.

Depression and anxiety reached its peak in October 1965, when I was thirty-five. At times, I would weep all the way home from work. I felt boxed in, with no way of escape. I would hold to this or that promise from God, hoping that I might find an answer to my plight.

On the night of October 25, I was at the point where I knew that I could not go on one more day. I was back on medication for pains in the back of my head. Had I not been a Christian, suicide would have been the only option.

It was at that point that the Spirit of God intervened in my life as, late that night, I was reading Galatians 2:20: "I am crucified with Christ." I had given up hope of help from God or anyone else, but God was gracious and sovereignly moved in my life that night and released me from all the anxiety, depression, pain in my head, and the inferiority feelings of a lifetime.

This feeling of total freedom lasted a day or two. Then some of the old feelings settled back in, and I had to learn a process the Bible calls "walking in the Spirit." Beyond the first step of being "filled with the Spirit," I had to learn to continue the process of allowing the Holy Spirit to have control of my life.

Since I didn't have anyone to disciple me in this new way of life, for the next couple of years I was up and down spiritually. During the first year, I read as many as a hundred books, including biographies and autobiographies, on the subject of the abundant life. I also spent many hours studying Paul's epistles to gain a theological understanding of what God had done in my life.

About two years later, it occurred to me that if God could set me free from my emotional disturbances, he could do the same for others. It seemed that the field of counseling would give me the means to share some of these answers. So I enrolled in a master's program in counseling at the University of Colorado, though its counseling program, as you might expect, was not noted for the spiritual content.

As I was praying about this decision to enter the counseling ministry, the Lord gave me two verses from Isaiah:

> And if thou draw out thy soul to the hungry, and satisfy the afflicted soul; then shall thy light rise in obscurity, and thy darkness be as the noon day: and the Lord shall guide thee continually, and satisfy thy soul in drought, and make fat thy bones: and thou shalt be like a watered garden, and like a spring of water, whose waters fail not. (Isa. 58:10-11)

I completed the master's program in December 1969, and God sovereignly provided a layoff from my position in the aerospace industry in January. In February 1970, I began the counseling ministry and at the same time began a doctoral program at the University of Northern Colorado, where I was allowed to design an innovative program that would integrate the spiritual and psychological dimensions of man. My study program would lead to a Doctor of Education in *Spirituotherapy*, as I chose to call it.

Atheists, agnostics, and Jewish professors proved to be more helpful to me than some Christians, who would try to force me into a system that omitted or deemphasized the effect that our relationship to the cross of Christ is to have on our lives. Even today, some Christians oppose these teachings, and I am trying to learn not to be defensive.

The cross of Christ, however, has never been a place where many people gather for fellowship, nor will it ever be. Those who have embraced the cross and its teachings don't think of themselves as having "arrived," except at the bottom. The cross in the life of the believer involves brokenness and suffering, just as it did for our Lord. Since pastors, counselors, psychologists, and psychiatrists are people, just like the rest of us, their road to victory over the flesh must be the same as ours.

There is such thing as an "end run" around the cross. None of us is greater than his Master, and all must go the way of the cross if we are to have victory in our Christian experience. Until believers understand this, they will continue to resist the message that holds that life must come out of death and victory out of defeat, whether in counseling or in any other kind of ministry.

What I learned during those days in 1965 was that the experience of the cross is an ongoing process. God allowed many things to come into my life during those days and since to contribute to my spiritual growth. I learned that we are all in the process of *becoming* in experience who we *already are* in Christ by position. Until we are one day with him, we will have to continue dealing with sin, in the world and in ourselves.

REJECTION AND ITS EFFECTS

As with all approaches to counseling, there has been continuing development over the years. As I began in 1970, I routinely took a life history of the counselee as part of the intake interview. As I did, I discovered a common thread running through the lives of those with whom I worked—a story of *rejection*. Some had been overtly, verbally or physically, rejected by their parents or some other significant person in their lives. Others were rejected in more subtle ways.

Those who have been openly rejected by their parents may understand to some degree the anger and distrust that resulted. However, most of these people did not always connect their present emotional and social maladjustment with the traumatic events of their childhood.

Those who had been rejected in subtle ways may have just as much emotional damage but be unaware of the source. Some heard their parents say that they were not wanted (overt rejection), while others as infants were given away by the parents through adoption. Adopted people, for instance, have been rejected by definition. Though the natural parents may have had no choice, the adopted child often thinks there was (and is) something wrong with him or her. Others were rejected but didn't see it at the time as rejection.

By *rejection* I mean "the absence of meaningful love." Being rejected doesn't mean there is no love involved, but that, for one reason or another, it is not fulfilling or edifying love. *The result of rejection is usually the impaired ability to give and receive love.*

People feel rejection for many reasons, such as from overprotection, performance-based acceptance, the premature death of parents, extended hospitalization in infancy, and from being the sex opposite what the parents wanted. Sometimes the rejection is subtle, sometimes unintentional, unrecognized, even unavoidable, or all of the above.

The *overprotected child* is not allowed to make decisions appropriate to his own age, so he doesn't develop confidence in himself or in his decision-making ability. By default, he is being told he is not capable of making decisions. And, deeming himself to be inferior, he develops an inferiority complex. His parents love him so much they do everything for him except allow him to become a person! Obviously, it is unintentional, and it is usually unknown, both to the parent and the child.

The overprotected (spoiled) child often becomes ambivalent

toward his parents. He loves them for what they do *for* him but resents them for what they do *to* him. Since he usually doesn't know what they did to him, he feels and thinks that he resents them for no cause, and feels guilty because of his feelings of resentment and his lack of appreciation. An "only child" is more likely to be overprotected than one from a family of several children.

The child who is loved for what he *does* rather than for what he *is* (performance-based acceptance) also feels rejected. His good performance is accepted, but his person is rejected.

One who loses his parents through death or divorce prior to his conscious memory experiences rejection that is perceived or felt but may never be understood. In similar manner, an infant who is in an incubator for an extended period of time has love withdrawn through no fault of the parents. However, it may leave emotional scars in the child.

One woman with whom I spoke, who had been in an incubator for the first three months of her life, could not accept the fact that her parents loved her at all until she was twenty-three years old. Obviously, she was not lying there in the incubator thinking that her parents hated her; but the void that was built into her emotions over the time spent in the incubator prevented her from *receiving* her parents' love, which was there in abundance. She received love but *perceived* or felt rejection.

An infant loses a primary source of love and acceptance if his parents are taken away through death. And, though it was no one's fault, the effects on interpersonal relationships can carry over into adulthood. Since the child has lost a trusted parent, the child in adulthood may find it hard to trust anyone. One fourteen-year-old boy, whose father and brother were killed in an auto accident and his mother seriously injured when he was six, was unable to attend school and studied under a teacher who came to his home. When I talked to him about surrendering everything to Christ, he grabbed his abdomen as if I had stabbed him with a knife. He asked, "Do you have an antacid?" He said he had been holding himself together and holding in his feelings for nine years and couldn't let go.

A person who suffers from rejection will often reject himself in some facet of his personality, sometimes in a socially acceptable way and sometimes not, especially when he tries to compensate for the unhealthy emotions that plague him. The effects of rejection on the personality vary, depending on the severity and duration of the rejection and the age of the person when it occurs. Sometimes a grandparent or another special person in the child's life can lessen the effects of the rejection.

A rejected person not only will reject himself but will also reject others, even marriage partners. Such a person also tends to blame others for problems in the relationship, absolving himself or herself from responsibility.

Some rejected people have trouble accepting and discharging responsibilities. Such a person would rather not try something than to try and fail, since the failure will cause him to feel even worse about himself. One such man, a chemical engineer who was doing a creditable job, felt himself a failure as a person and an employee. One day his supervisor came to him and said, "We are going to give you a $5,000 per year increase in salary and an automobile." John replied, "That does it! I quit!" He turned on his heel and walked out of the office. His internal conflicts were so severe, he felt he couldn't possibly accept any further responsibility.

The cause and effects of rejection are covered more fully in my book entitled *The Rejection Syndrome* (Tyndale House, 1982).

The answer to rejection is *acceptance*. Human acceptance, however, will not heal the damaged emotions after rejection has done its dirty work. It does help, and often it will be the only help available, but the experience of being accepted in Christ is the only true curative.

IDENTITY

The importance of *identity* and the many ways it affects the whole of our existence is another concept that has become a part of my counseling during the past years. It is important because that which a person sees as his identity, or the identity he would *like* to make work for him, will determine where he looks for acceptance.

Most believers live with an identity that has been assigned to them, either positive or negative, depending on the extent of rejection, or with an identity they have built for themselves. Many are so-called "self-made" men and women, and end up being dissatisfied with the job they have done. Usually the identity has been based on things, money, people, power, and accomplishments or lack of them. Identity based on temporal things will naturally be subject to change without notice.

The Apostle Paul differentiated between our fleshly identity and our spiritual identity, what we are as a result of human resources and what we are through the Holy Spirit's power. Again, as it was for the problem of rejection, the cure for an unacceptable fleshly identity is a true spiritual identity, which only a proper relationship to Christ can give us.

In the flesh, our natural resources, we have been programmed in certain directions by the teaching and experiences we have had. Some are programmed so that their identity is fulfilled through accumulation of money and things; others are programmed toward success in business or some other achievements. Some are programmed toward sensuality, some even toward religious pursuits.

For the believer, all of these are false and unsatisfactory identities, since our true identity is based on who we are in Christ. Many believers, however, never seem to discover their true identity until they get to glory. David Needham deals with this vital truth in his book *Birthright* (Multnomah, 1982). The problem is that many people are living out of the wrong identity—the one shaped by being "conformed to this world" rather than being "transformed by the renewing of [their] minds" (Rom. 12:2).

The answer to the problem, though many have called such a suggestion "overly simplistic," is in exchanging the identity based on our personal history and the influence of indwelling sin for our perfect identity in Christ. Such a transaction truly takes a miracle, but it is the kind of miracle in which the Holy Spirit majors. The Holy Spirit does not enter our lives to patch up our old identities but to put into effect our true identity as redeemed children of the King of kings. Paul described this work within us:

> That the God of our Lord Jesus Christ, the Father of glory, may give unto you the spirit of wisdom and revelation in the knowledge of him: the eyes of your understanding being enlightened; that ye may know what is the hope of his calling, and what the riches of the glory of his inheritance in the saints, and what is the exceeding greatness of his power to us-ward who believe, according to the working of his mighty power, which he wrought in Christ, when he raised him from the dead, and set him at his own right hand in the heavenly places. (Eph. 1:17-20)

These verses show that the same power God used in raising Jesus from the dead is operative in us as we place our faith in what was accomplished through Christ's resurrection. Paul wrote, "For if, when we were enemies, we were reconciled to God by the death of his Son, much more, being reconciled, we shall be saved by his life" (Rom. 5:10).

Our identity is based on who we are in Christ and it is to be claimed by faith—not by works, ours or any other's. We shed the trappings of the past by exchanging our fleshly identity for the Christ-life, by exchanging a life of defeat for a life of victory. Jesus told his followers, "If any man will come after me, let him deny himself, and take up his cross daily, and follow me" (Luke 9:23). Many have a faulty notion of what "self" and "denying self" really is. Some think that denying themselves some worldly pleasures will fulfill this command. Others think that "taking up the cross" is bearing some burden such as caring for a severely handicapped child. Obviously, it is difficult to deny ourselves if we don't know what "self" is.

What does it mean to embrace our own old identity, the one we are to deny if we are to exchange it for our new identity in Christ? As an analogy, suppose that you or someone you know is fifteen years old, unmarried, and pregnant. Abortion is not a consideration, and the firm decision has been made to give the baby up for adoption. Would you recommend that a young lady in such a situation see the baby prior to relinquishing it or not? In either case, what would be your rationale for the choice you have made?

It would be easier to have the baby and leave the hospital without having seen it and, thus, avoid the trauma of separation. Or, would it? At the time, it would seem easier, but has the reality of the situation been faced? Did you ever try to give away something you never had? Without having seen the baby, there is a sense of unreality about the whole incident. Yes, the baby has been carried in the womb, but there is a difference between this and holding the baby and owning it. Once it is held and owned and loved for a day or so and then given to the adoptive parents, the reality hits with full force. Then it is possible to go through the grief process, the separation anxiety, or whatever other names could be given to the traumatic loss experienced by the young mother.

Each of us needs to ask the question, "Have I owned my 'baby,' or is there still a sense of unreality about the identity out of which I live?" Each of us must define our identity and look at it squarely to understand that which we must lose if we are to live out our true identity in the Lord Jesus Christ. We must "lose our baby," which has been in the formation state for a lifetime if we are to know the joy, the blessing of our new identity as accepted and dearly loved children of God in Christ.

> Then said Jesus unto his disciples, If any man will come after me, let him deny himself, and take up his cross, and follow me. For whosoever will save his life shall lose it: and whosoever will lose his life for my sake shall find it. (Matt. 16:24-25)

TWO
HOW
SPIRITUOTHERAPY
WORKS

In order to understand ourselves, it is necessary that we have a clear conception of how we are made up and how we function. Our thoughts, feelings, and behaviors derive from an identity that we may not have recognized, and our motivation for present actions and reactions are a function of that identity. Or, to put it another way, the identity we have been assigned by others or the one that we have built for ourselves, positive or negative, will have a great influence on the decisions we make and the way we relate to others.

Since we are, at the core, spiritual beings, it behooves us to know what our spiritual identity is and the influence that Spirit-given knowledge can have on our psychological and social functioning. Over the years, it has proven extremely helpful to most of those with whom I have counseled to understand the makeup or constituency of man, known in theological circles as biblical anthropology. Obviously, there are many views on this vital matter, but the discussions here will be limited to what the New Testament seems to support.

There are two major Scripture references that suggest that man is made up of three parts—body, soul, and spirit (the trichotomy view)—but other references also seem to support the assertion that man has a spirit that functions as a separate entity (1 Thess.

5:23; Heb. 4:12). A common way of looking at man is as being material and immaterial. These two component parts are sometimes called body and soul, or body and mind (the dichotomy view). But this latter view does not allow for a spirit in man, even though it would be taught that man functions spiritually. Although man functions somewhat like members of the animal kingdom, though on a higher psychological level, I believe that it is the spirit of man that makes him intrinsically different from animals.

It is important to use a model that accords with Scripture when we try to explain the psychological and spiritual functions of man and that we use biblical terminology rather than using a purely psychological model. Otherwise, we come up with some vague generalities that will not support a true integration of psychology and theology. Paul wrote, "And the very God of peace sanctify you wholly; and I pray God your whole spirit and soul and body be preserved blameless until the coming of our Lord Jesus Christ" (1 Thess. 5:23). The writer of Hebrews wrote, "For the word of God is quick, and powerful, and sharper than any two-edged sword, piercing even to the dividing asunder of soul and spirit, and of the joints and marrow, and is a discerner of the thoughts and intents of the heart" (Heb. 4:12).

Other biblical references to the soul and spirit are not so definitive, but many allude to the existence of the soul and the spirit as separate entities. For example, when the Lord Jesus was on the cross he, being in the body, chose—an act of the soul—to dismiss his spirit. Paul wrote, "But he that is joined to the Lord is one spirit" (1 Cor. 6:17). Obviously, this speaks of a union of the spirit as opposed to a union of the soul. Drawing on the language of Scripture, we might say that man *is* a spirit, that he *has* a soul, and that he *lives in* a body. *It is vital that this entire book be read with this understanding, since some statements could be misconstrued if applied to any other than a trichotomous (tripartite) view of man.*

Since the prime concern of this book is to discover our true identity and to see a spiritual resolution for psychological and interpersonal symptoms, we need to see how the concept of identity relates to man. To do this, we need to begin with Adam, since that is where it all began! Adam had a perfect identity, and he found his entire meaning in his relationship with God. The following diagram shows his makeup of spirit, soul, and body. In Genesis we read that man (Adam) was created in the image of God (1:26). He was created innocent and remained in this condition, able to communicate with God until the Fall. Though the spirit of Adam is not mentioned specifically, we read, "The Lord God formed man of the dust of the ground, and breathed into his nostrils the breath of life (or lives), and man became a living soul" (2:7).

DIAGRAM 1
ADAM PRIOR TO THE FALL

The spirit at creation was not contaminated with sin, and Adam functioned on a supernatural level in naming the animals and completing all the other tasks God gave him. The arrow (or arc) inside the circle depicts interaction between spirit, soul, and body, with no conflict. The arrows toward the outside indicate interaction with God as well as mankind and with the environment.

The arrows within this diagram depict the interrelationships of spirit, soul, and body. These along with other terms used or implied in the Scriptures are adequate to explain the totality of man and his intrapersonal and interpersonal functions.

God told Adam, "But of the tree of the knowledge of good and evil, thou shalt not eat of it: for in the day that thou eatest thereof thou shalt surely die" (Gen. 2:17). Since they did eat (Gen. 3:6), we know that some kind of death took place that day. Obviously, it was not physical death. Their souls continued to function psychologically. As a result of their sin, physical death did one day occur; but some kind of death took place that day. It could only have been a spiritual death, and the remainder of the Bible addresses itself to the consequences of that event. The next diagram shows what man was like after the Fall.

In the diagrams, you will note that the *soul* might be called our self-consciousness or the personality through which we relate to others—actually our psychological makeup. The *spirit* is our God-consciousness, or the facet of our makeup by which we relate to God. The *body*, of course, is the means by which we relate to the world and our environment through our five senses. In summary, we relate to others through our soul, to God through our spirit, and to our environment through our body. The soul is composed of mind (or intellect), the emotions (or affections), and the will (or volition). The *spirit* has similar functions but it will not be helpful to discuss them at this point.

As depicted by the arrow between body and soul (Diagram 2), there can be physical problems such as an endocrine imbalance or other ailments that can have an adverse effect on our emotional state. Likewise, we can suffer from long-standing psychological symptoms that affect our spiritual life and hamper our walk with God. Being spiritually maladjusted will produce or amplify existing psychological symptoms. So we can have difficulties in any of the three areas that may, in turn, have an adverse effect on another area. It will be necessary to refer constantly to the wheel diagram as we proceed to differentiate the functions of spirit, soul, and body and the understandings we should have regarding needs and problems in each area.

Of course, the first and prime consideration is our relationship with God. Unless and until a personal relationship is established, the content of this book is just so much rhetoric. That initial personal relationship and all that pertains to it have to do with the *spirit* and are explained in terms of our *salvation*.

DIAGRAM 2

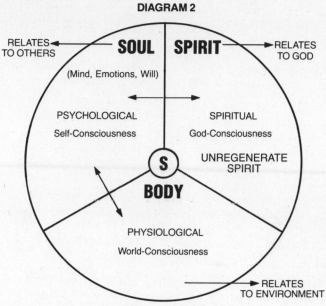

MAN—A TRI-UNITY

As you will note, there is now a smaller circle in the center to depict the fact that man after the Fall was *flesh,* meaning that from that point on he lived a self-centered life. Later in Genesis we read, "And the Lord said, My spirit shall not always strive with man, for he also is flesh" (6:3).

Throughout this book, the words *flesh* and *self* will be used interchangeably when referring to the control center of a believer living out of his own resources. When the word *self* is used, it should not be understood as meaning the same as *personality,* for example.

In the center of the circle is the letter S (self), referring to the fact that Adam positionally became *flesh* or self-centered and that each of us is born into the world with the same dilemma (Rom. 5:12). Later we will see that this self-centered position is used of the believer as a *condition.* At the Fall, Adam and Eve's identity shifted from God to themselves in relation to Satan. Their problem afterward was not so much the individual acts of sin they committed as the fact that they were now in an entirely different sphere of life, or death, as the case may be. Though they each had a functioning spirit, they now functioned toward Satan instead of God. We might say that the *spirit was dead to God and alive to Satan.*

The initial personal relationship and some of its outworkings are listed under "Spirit," and some are explained as follows:

SALVATION

Variously defined as conversion to Christ, being born again, being saved, trusting Christ as Savior and Lord, accepting Christ, receiving Christ, salvation is entering into a personal relationship with God through personal faith in Jesus Christ. Unless the Lord Jesus Christ is *in* our life, obviously, he cannot make the necessary changes. His entrance into the life brings about a spiritual birth that is only the beginning of our life in Christ. Before we trust the Lord Jesus Christ in a personal surrender, the Holy Spirit must convince us that we are *born* sinners.

Paul concluded, "Wherefore, as by one man [Adam] sin entered into the world, and death by sin; and so death passed upon all men, for that all have sinned" (Rom. 5:12). Since we are born with a sinful nature, or "old man" (NASB; NIV), we naturally commit sins. Paul wrote, "All have sinned and come short of the glory of God" (Rom. 3:23).

The penalty for sin is stated: "For the wages of sin is death; but the gift of God is eternal life through Jesus Christ our Lord" (Rom. 6:23). The death penalty must be paid, and it *has* been paid: "But God commendeth [exhibits or proves] his love toward us, in that, while we were yet sinners, Christ died for us" (Rom. 5:8).

When we are ready to admit that we are ungodly and to believe on the Lord Jesus Christ, then we will be justified and counted righteous in God's sight. "But to him that worketh not, but believeth on him that justifieth the ungodly, his faith is counted for righteousness" (Rom. 4:5). The method is very simple. We merely believe what the Bible says about us (that we are ungodly sinners), and we also believe what the Bible says about the Lord Jesus (that he was and is God, that he died for our sins, and that he rose from the dead). This is very clearly stated in Scripture: "That if thou shalt confess with thy mouth the Lord Jesus, and shalt believe in thine heart that God hath raised him from the dead, thou shalt be saved. For with the heart man believeth unto righteousness, and with the mouth confession is made unto salvation" (Rom. 10:9-10).

After we hear and believe, we must call upon God in prayer: "For whoever shall call upon the name of the Lord shall be saved" (Rom. 10:13). A simple prayer will do, such as: "Dear God, I know I am a sinner. I believe that you sent your Son, the Lord Jesus Christ, to die for my sins, that he was buried, and that he rose from the dead. I surrender now and turn from a life of sin and trust the Lord Jesus Christ to forgive my sins and to be my life. Thank you for saving me, for Jesus' sake. Amen."

Upon the basis of his infallible Word, he saves us when we believe and call upon him. After we have settled the question of salvation in our lives, we must learn to rejoice in the *assurance* that God has done what he said he would do.

ASSURANCE

It is possible to be saved but not be assured of that salvation. Our assurance must be based on the facts of Scripture rather than on fluctuating feelings. The person who is sometimes labeled *neurotic* most often wants to feel something rather than believe it, and his style of living is to distort reality. As a result, there is no reason for him to believe that his feelings will be trustworthy in the matter of salvation.

There is a profound difference between doubting one's salvation (mental) and feeling unsaved (emotional). Most people who lack assurance are those who *feel* unsaved. However, most of us do not make a distinction between the functions of the mind and the emotions. Neither do most personnel workers, who attempt to help those who lack assurance. The appeal is made to the mind with the facts of the gospel when the emotions are really the cause of the confusion. When the emotions are being controlled by lies the person has been believing, there is no way the emotions will ever agree with truth. Therefore, a person may *know* (mental) he is saved and never doubt his salvation and yet *feel* (emotional) unsaved for a lifetime.

A veteran missionary who had felt unsaved off and on for more than a quarter century was greatly relieved upon being shown this distinction. Though the feelings were not changed immediately, an understanding of the problem gave new light. The testimony to a group of missionaries the following day was, "Today I *know* I am saved and I don't care whether I *feel* saved or not!"

The Bible, speaking to believers, tell us that we are to *know* that we have eternal life (1 John 5:13). It is not at all presumptuous to take God at his Word and simply rest in it. We can establish our assurance only by accepting God's Word for what it is. After we have assurance of our salvation, we can go on to finding *security* in that fact.

SECURITY

Our relationship with him is unbreakable—eternal. We are secure in that relationship, and we cannot have assurance if we are not secure and confident that this relationship is lasting. Paul wrote, "your life is hid with Christ in God" (Col. 3:3). If we do not realize this, our assurance cannot be solid because we will be afraid of losing our salvation. And if we are afraid we will lose it, we will struggle to do something in order to maintain it, such as good works. As a result, we cease to live trusting in God's grace and begin to live again trusting in our obedience to the law for our salvation. This Paul described as "falling from grace" (Gal. 5:4). Many evangelical Christians live this way—saved by grace but, by practical outworking, still bound by the law.

Unless a person has his security nailed down, he is unlikely to mature in his relationship with Jesus Christ. Of course, assurance and security really go hand in hand. You cannot experience one to any great degree without the other.

ACCEPTANCE

Some accept the Lord Jesus Christ as personal Savior and Lord and then spend the rest of their lives trying to get him to accept them. Of course, this is a futile effort because the Scriptures assure us that "we are accepted in the beloved [Christ]" (Eph. 1:6). Our being accepted by Christ doesn't depend on our good works or how much we read the Bible or how much we go to church or any other effort we may expend. Our acceptance is rooted solely in his finished work at Calvary—not our work *for* him. Salvation is by grace from start to finish. Acceptance is by grace, too. God accepts his Son; and since we are in his Son, "accepted in the beloved," he accepts us as well.

Many today have difficulty believing that their parents accept them or that their peers accept them. In fact, many persons feel that no one really accepts them. As a result, they come to feel that God relates to them in the same manner. If they are not fit for other people to accept, why should God accept them? Of course, this isn't the case. But if a person *feels* that way, to him this perception will govern his behavior.

Then what is the answer? He must come to the place where he, through the illumination of the Holy Spirit, realizes that he is accepted. He *is* acceptable, not because of anything he has done, but because of the great things the Lord Jesus Christ has done. When he was saved—when he trusted the Lord Jesus Christ as his personal Savior—he was put *into* Christ (1 Cor. 1:30). Having been put into Christ, he is accepted by God *in Christ*. In this, as in the initial salvation experience, we must take God at his word and believe what he says regardless of how we may feel about it. As we begin to take him at his word, our feelings begin to line up with the facts.

Acceptance by God and identification with Christ in death, burial, and resurrection are much like opposite sides of a coin. When one is realized in experience, the other will be also. A case in point is that of a woman who had been filled with extreme hostility. She had tried psychiatric treatment before coming to our Grace Fellowship office. After approximately three counseling interviews and attendance at three lectures I gave, God set her free. She had intellectually understood the principles set forth in this book when on Saturday night she began to meditate on Galatians 2:20: "I am crucified with Christ." On Sunday morning, as she was driving to church, she was singing the hymn, "Calvary Love." As she sang the refrain, "I long to be worthy of Calvary love," the Holy Spirit dealt with her. She realized that *in Christ she was worthy*. She began to weep and cry out, "I am accepted. I am acceptable!" The question of her acceptance was settled as was the extreme hostility. No longer was she dominated by psychological difficulties that had beset her since childhood.

TOTAL COMMITMENT

Salvation, assurance, security, and acceptance leave us still lacking in one important point—total commitment. Consecration, dedication, surrender, submission, and other terms are used to denote this vital step in the Christian's life. It is necessary to define the term as we will be using it throughout this book.

Paul wrote, "I beseech you therefore, brethren, by the mercies of God, that ye present your bodies a living sacrifice, holy, acceptable unto God, which is your reasonable service" (Rom. 12:1). Total commitment, according to this verse, is something *we* can do. It is our "reasonable service." It is an act of the will by which we tell our Father than we want more than anything else in this world to have his will accomplished in our lives, whatever that means. We may not know his specific purpose in this life for us. But after we have wholly committed our lives to him, he begins to bring it to pass (Ps. 37:5).

Total surrender is essential to total usefulness. Occasionally, a person accepts the Lord Jesus Christ as Savior and makes him Lord of his life at the beginning. This is what should happen in all conversions. One should not accept Jesus Christ as Savior and then wait ten or fifteen years to yield completely to him. This should take place the day a person accepts Christ. When it doesn't, a person has to see the futility of running his own life—or ruining it, as is frequently the case—and come to the place where he is ready to say, "Lord, I want to take my hands off my life. I want you to run it."

This decision is comparable to the ceremony in which a man and woman are joined in marriage. Each of them says, by an act of the will, "I do." Based upon this act of their wills, before God and a minister, they are pronounced man and wife. They have met the legal requirements for marriage. The act of the will has been made, but they are still not man and wife until the marriage union is consummated. With an act of the will they have made a decision that changes the entire course of their lives. But neither of them feels automatically like a wife or a husband. The total commitment to the Lord is much the same, in which, by an act of our will, we say, "I do." or "I will." "Whatever you want, your will be done in my life."

Our wills have been exercised, but usually our lives are not miraculously transformed at that time, although some persons' are. A few who come for counseling are at the point where there is no way out. When they come through in a complete surrender, God consummates the transformation in the life immediately or in a very short time. But in many cases, once this surrender is made, with or without emotion, there is little observable change. From that point, the responsibility is turned over to God, and he begins to bring about a consummation of his purpose and plan in their lives.

Looking back to Romans 12:1, we surrender our lives as a "living sacrifice." This hearkens back to the Old Testament sacrifice, which was a lamb placed on the altar. The lamb had no choice. Someone else put him there. As he was bound on the altar, he was totally committed by someone else to be the sacrifice. He could not say to the priest, "Now, listen, do anything to me, but don't cut my throat!" That was *exactly* what the priests had in mind. The lamb was totally under the control of another.

But this is exactly what our surrender must be if our faithful

High Priest is to bring about the consummation in our lives, by which we will experience the fullness of our union with Jesus Christ. Unlike the lamb, we have control, but we relinquish it, submitting ourselves to be placed on the altar.

DIAGRAM 3

In the salvation experience referred to earlier, on our invitation Christ enters into our spirit. This is represented by the C in the lower part of Diagram 3. Christ is in the life, but he can be *in* the life without being the *center* of the life. Tragically, this is true of a great many Christians. In fact, that person may be so busy with life, that Christ might remain on the periphery. Another person may be so busy working *for* the Lord that he doesn't have time to spend *with* him. As a result, Christ is not central in the life. But because of the trials and adversities that God permits in our lives, we may realize that we need Christ in the center of our lives—not off on the periphery somewhere. If Christ is not the center of our lives, something else is. The thing or person that is so important that it becomes the motivating force of our lives is referred to as the *center* of the life.

The S in the center of the circle might, for instance, represent *some thing*, such as a home or a car or some other thing that we feel would really make us happy. Usually, we strive and struggle to get these things, and once the newness wears off we find we have won a hollow victory.

The center might be occupied by *some person*—a father, a mother, a husband, a wife, a child, a boyfriend, or a girlfriend— some person in our lives we seek to please or satisfy, or to satisfy us, so that we can feel good about ourselves. This might be either a positive or a negative orientation. For instance, one or both of our parents could cause us to feel a certain way about ourselves. Even though they might be hundreds of miles away or deceased, we still feel about ourselves the way they caused us to feel.

The S in the center might be *success,* however we define it in our lives. A businessman could be struggling to get to the top, to become the president of the company. A minister may seek success by struggling to work, work, work to get to a place where he can have a more influential ministry or a larger church. Success for a student might be making all A's. Regardless of the manner chosen, the motivating force in some lives is success.

For a sex deviate, it might be that *sex* is the most important thing in life, in that his whole life is centered around it. For some it might be *drugs* and the experience to be derived from them. A heroin addict might consider the most important thing in life as getting another fix, so that becomes his all-consuming passion. For some, especially in the materialistic American culture, the most important thing is *money* and the things money can buy. But all of these manifestations represent things *we* want or something that *we* think will give *us* satisfaction. All of these S's may be summed up in the term *self* (or flesh). (As I mentioned earlier, *self* in the way it is being used in this book is not synonymous with *personality.* One renowned Christian psychologist erroneously claimed that I teach the annihilation of the personality— thus the reason for this disclaimer.)

Someone has said that we can drop the *h* from the word *flesh,* spell it backwards, and we have the word *self.* It is correct to use the word *self* as a synonym for the *soul*—the mind, emotions, and will—that which constitutes us as unique individuals. The soul, in and of itself, is neutral. Whatever is placed in the center,

S or *C*, becomes the driving force that empowers the soul, determining its attitudes and actions and the ultimate worth of that which results. Self in the center of the life means *we* are in control or, at least, trying to be. Of course, according to Jeremiah, no one is able by himself to control his own life: "It is not in man that walketh to direct his steps" (Jer. 10:23). We are designed so that, if we will give our volitional consent, God will control our spirit, our spirit will then control our soul, and our soul will control our body. This is God's plan; and for it to work, Christ must be at the control center. We should be Christ-centered rather than self-centered. But many Christians, even those in full-time Christian work, still find that they are still doing it *for him* rather than his doing it *through him*.

Hudson Taylor was an example of this. As a young man, he was saved and called into the ministry. After receiving his theological and medical training, he went to the mission field and was used of God to found the China Inland Mission (now Overseas Missionary Fellowship). He went out completely in faith, totally dependent upon God to supply every need, financial and otherwise. God blessed Hudson Taylor's work and sent out many missionaries who also had to be completely dependent on God. But Taylor was on the mission field between ten and fifteen years before he finally came to the end of Hudson Taylor and all his own resources and quit trying to work *for* God. Then Christ began to live and work *through* him.

God does not want us to work *for* him, to witness *for* him, to live *for* him. He wants to get *self* out of the way so he can work through us. This is the lesson that many Christians never learn. Usually, it is only learned through hardship, trial, affliction, and suffering to the point where we deal with self. Self, then, is no longer the center of our life. Our mind and emotions are controlled by the indwelling Christ as we will or reckon upon our resources in him. Until this process is completed, self is in control; and we use our own will and mind to run our lives, instead of only using them in the *doing* role. In other words, we are *doing* in order to *be* rather than *being* in order to *do*. As a result, we are less effective in living. If God is running our lives, then our mind, emotions, and will are free to serve his purposes unhampered by the additional duties of trying to decide how we should live our lives. As long as self is in control, the functions of the soul will operate in direct correspondence to the historical events that have characterized our maturation, and these may be worsened by the ways we have attempted to meet our own needs.

SOUL

Looking now at the psychological (or "soul") functions, we will consider some needs and difficulties a person may face.

DIAGRAM 4

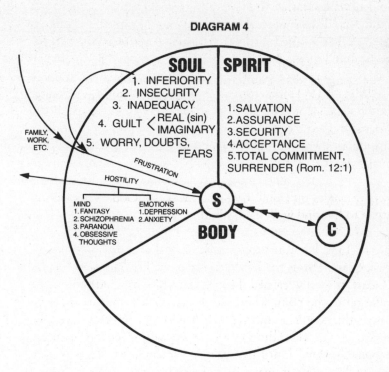

First of all, let us consider the often-used term *inferiority,* a feeling that plagues most of us in some areas of our lives. With some people, feelings of inferiority are so intense that personal relationships are hampered. It can hinder their work to the point that, when assignments are given to them, they have to fight to get to the place, finally, where they can begin the task. Once they get started, they usually do an exceptional job; but they still *feel* they cannot achieve. Their minds tell them one thing, and their feelings tell them another. Usually, they know intellectually that they are not inferior; but they feel that they are. Such a conflict can lead to serious emotional problems, as it did for me, because of the methods used to compensate for it.

Feelings of *insecurity* present another problem. Some people are filled with fears and doubts about themselves and what is going to happen next. Such people often must contend with the feeling that something terrible is going to happen to them. They cannot relax and have that good feeling inside because of the apprehensions which, in turn, spawn other symptoms. Insecurity in the marriage relationship can give rise to jealousy and jealousy to accusations, and the cycle often goes on until divorce results. Insecurity in the work relationship causes people to fear the loss of jobs or of demotion, which causes workers to be ineffective and brings about the very results they feared. One pastor's wife was so jealous that he couldn't have even an eighty-year-old secretary—not because of any indiscretions on his part but solely because of his wife's insecurity.

Feelings of *inadequacy*, another common problem, can take two forms—feelings of personal inadequacy or the feelings of inadequacy in certain situations. Feelings of personal inadequacy, like feelings of inferiority, make people think, in almost any situation, that they are incapable of coping with life. Others feel inadequate in certain situations. For instance, a person might feel inadequate in his home, in a family role, but he might feel totally adequate on the job. He might be a professional man, or an executive in a company, and his work is held in high esteem. He is admired, so he feels wonderful and stays overtime, possibly working ten or twelve hours a day. In the home relationship, he cannot get along with his wife or his children, so he stays at work and becomes a loyal company man. It is not necessarily because he likes the work so much but because he cannot make it at home. The converse could be true, where a person feels protected and safe at home, but he has fear in his employment because he is really not making a success of it.

A fourth bad feeling is *guilt*, and again there are two forms of it. The first is *real guilt*, and we must face it as such. We must not try to explain it away or cover it and call it "guilt feelings," but show it to be the result of sin, just as the Word of God proclaims it to be. The only cure for real guilt and its cause, sin, is forgiveness and cleansing through the blood of Jesus Christ. John wrote, "If we confess our sins, he is faithful and just to forgive us our sins, and to cleanse us from all unrighteousness" (1 John 1:9). This is the only way real guilt can be put away. Of course, all sin and guilt is dealt with when we are saved, when we trust Jesus Christ. But afterward, the sin that crops up in our lives must be dealt with by acknowledging it to God and forsaking it. If we do this, he forgives and cleanses us, as he promised in 1 John 1:9.

Apart from the real guilt that all of us have, from time to time, many suffer from *imaginary guilt*, which feels exactly the same as real guilt. We can confess and confess and confess and still be plagued with the problem. Many think because of these feelings that they have committed the unpardonable sin or that there is some sin that they just cannot uncover. They do not know what it is, but they think that if they could just find it and confess it they would be free.

Imaginary guilt may spring from a lack of love and acceptance. As an unwanted child, a person may feel no deep sense of belonging. Sometimes the child is told that he is unwanted while another merely senses it. As a result, the person becomes conscience-smitten for just being there, feeling he is the cause of all the problems around him. If he were out of the picture, he thinks, the family would be fine. He feels guilty for even being a person.

Such imagined guilt can persist throughout life. Understanding the problem is the first step in turning it over to the Lord. Experiencing God's acceptance is the antidote to feelings of rejection.

We must consider also the general category of *worry, doubts, and fears.* When we have inner turmoil, we are prone to worry. God's Word admonishes us to "be anxious for nothing" (Phil. 4:6), but many don't know how to appropriate this truth, and they continue to worry about everything. When they do, they have various doubts—doubts that other people love them or doubts that God is real. They may doubt that he will meet their needs, and they begin to fret. Nagging doubts cause many kinds of fears, the fear of failure or a myriad of other forms. Fear is all-pervasive, and it can really wreck us. It can become an irrational fear, a phobia. The underlying cause is a faulty faith. In fact, all five of the preceding symptoms are indicative of a failure to trust in Christ and depend upon him fully.

There are people whose fears seem to have fears! The more the fears are compounded, the less space a person has in which to live. This may result in the inability to drive a car. Fear of people and crowds, *agoraphobia,* may cause a person to pull down the shades and become a prisoner in his own home.

When we have all these things going on inside and acting upon each other, inner turmoil results. The internal frustration is compounded by external stresses from family, work, and other adverse conditions. You will note on the wheel that we have encircled all five items and labeled the result as frustration. Such frustration has a direct bearing on *self.* The result can be illustrated by the striking of a golf ball. If the ball has a live center, it will react with the club head and travel a great distance. If the center is dead, not much is going to happen. If self is very much alive and the frustration comes in, the result may be hostility. Such an agitated person can strike something with his hand or want to throw something.

The problem arises in dealing with these feelings of hostility. The prime goal of some psychotherapists is to teach such a person how to handle his hostility, a futile effort, because as soon as the person learns how to handle it, the problem is going to pop up in another form. The problem is not in knowing how to handle it but in how to prevent it. The hostility is sometimes projected onto someone else (displaced hostility), usually a person who does not deserve it. The pressure is relieved to some extent by acting out hostility, but additional guilt is incurred, which serves to increase the frustration, and another hostile act is committed. On and on the cycle goes.

DIAGRAM 5

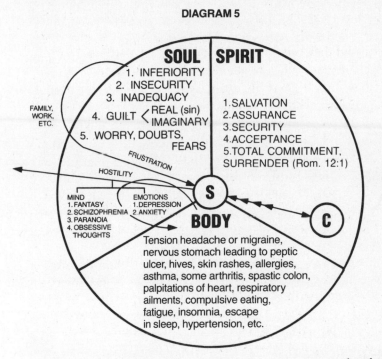

One form of psychotherapy advocates getting out the feelings—emotional catharsis—as a means of venting hostility. This is workable in the therapeutic climate, but not everyone has a safe situation in which to dump their hostility. Society at large does not accept negative feelings with tender loving care. Many people are filled with hostility who have no acceptable means of dealing with it. They cannot verbalize it satisfactorily, and they cannot exercise violence toward other people to get it out. They either keep all or some of it inside. When hostility is kept inside, the conflict can travel in either of two directions as shown on the diagram. It can affect our mind, our emotions, or both. If it influences the mind, there are several things that can happen.

One is *fantasy*. A person can spend his time thinking how he would *like* things to be. A little of this is acceptable because sometimes we do make our daydreams come true. But, if we live in a fantasy world, we are not effective in the real world. A person who is prone to this (and some who are not) might have a psychotic break and become *schizophrenic,* living in an unreal world. Such a person may have to be institutionalized and permitted to live in that unreal world because he is incapable of living in reality.

The person might become *paranoid* due to feelings of inadequacy or guilt. A person who feels inadequate usually blames his failures on someone else. This becomes a pattern, and he begins to believe his own lie. Eventually, he becomes certain that a person or group is really out to get him. This may also stem from guilt, the person feeling as if he should be punished. In his fantasy he imagines that someone intends him bodily harm. Instead of being completely out of touch with reality, he usually has well structured delusions, while in other areas of life he may be in touch with reality.

The person may also become *obsessed* with certain thoughts of which the person cannot rid himself. This problem sometimes results in obsessive compulsive behaviors such as the washing of hands to get some kind of relief from the anxiety. A good definition of obsessive thoughts is that a person's mind is putting on a sideshow to keep it off the main event. Eventually, this sideshow may be more troublesome than the problem it was intended to replace.

These aberrations are not necessarily mental illness, but they are mental symptoms of a deeper problem—self at the center of the life. Treating symptoms rarely effects a permanent cure. People can go to psychiatrists much or all of their lives for treatment of such symptoms. Some chronic schizophrenics *do* have a problem with their brain chemistry. But I contend that many of those who are diagnosed as schizophrenic are denying reality to protect themselves from situations, external or internal, they cannot face.

In addition to symptoms in the mind, the frustration can affect the emotions, another area of the soul. Or both the mind and emotions may be affected. A common effect on the emotions is *depression*. Hostility kept inward becomes depression. We push against ourselves. We take it out on ourselves instead of taking it out on someone else. We beat ourselves severely about the head and shoulders, which causes us to be depressed, anxious, and tied up in knots. A more homespun definition of depression is that of an internal temper tantrum. This can be simple depression or it can become more severe and be termed reactive depression or clinical depression. Still these are not, at their root, mental problems or real emotional problems. They are symptoms of a deeper problem. The problem is usually treated by attempting to rid the afflicted one of the anxiety and depression that has been bottled up inside.

This anxiety and depression is usually contained until it is no longer possible to restrict it to the domain of the soul. Then it manifests itself in the body as a psychosomatic or psychophysiological symptom. Many of these could be listed. It can be a tension headache that can become migraine, or it can be a nervous stomach and the ubiquitous antacid pills or a combination of antacids or tranquilizers. The nervous stomach is the breeding place for a peptic ulcer. Some other common ailments stemming from psychological conflict are hives, some forms of arthritis, asthma, skin rashes, spastic colon, palpitations of the heart, and respiratory ailments. It should be noted, however, that many of these ailments listed may also be true physiological problems that have nothing to do with psychological conflict. Physicians who have written on this subject estimate that 60 to 80 percent of their patients have ailments caused by psychological conflict. If a person has "the peace of God which passeth all understanding" (Phil. 4:7), he cannot continue to have unabated emotional conflict. Ultimately, these physical or psychosomatic symptoms are spiritual problems; since the only complete answer is spiritual, the problem must be spiritual as well.

To summarize, it is because *self* is at the center of the life that all of this conflict has developed and continues to grow. The problems may have been there since childhood, but the fact that they continue means that *self* is running the life. It may be a good self; it may be a bad self; it may be in between; but it is still self, and *self in control of the life is repugnant to God.*

In psychotherapy, of whatever persuasion, self is strengthened to cope with those problems. Herein lies the basic problem with psychotherapy. With enough psychotherapy, some of the symptoms will respond so that the person may become better adjusted, with the symptoms either diminishing or leaving. But, in order to cope with them, better defense mechanisms are built and more acceptable behaviors are learned; and self becomes stronger. Thus, when symptoms improve as a result of pure psychotherapy, the real problem, self-centeredness, *always* gets worse. This result is diametrically opposed to what God does, because God's way of dealing with *self* is that it must become weaker and weaker until its control is finally phased out. Self is reduced to nothing so that Christ can be everything. This is the process by which Christ becomes the center of the life, the basis for which is described in Diagrams 7-9.

When Christ is in control, self, or flesh, no longer holds sway. It is not permanently replaced; but the cross blocks the power of sin as we understand under the tutelage of the Holy Spirit, the truth of Romans 6:11: "Likewise reckon ye also yourselves to be dead indeed unto sin, but alive unto God through Jesus Christ our Lord." We are still a unique self or individual, empowered by the life of Christ within. On the positive side, we *do* still have a personality. But when Christ is in the center of the life, we have Christ in control. Paul wrote, "Let this mind be in you which was also in Christ Jesus" (Phil 2:5). He also wrote, "I can do all things through Christ which strengtheneth me" (Phil 4:3), and "But my God shall supply all your need according to his riches in glory, by Christ Jesus" (Phil 4:19). "All your needs" includes the emotional. And he will supply them not by a psychologist or a counselor but "by Christ Jesus."

When Christ is at the center of the life, he can meet all the needs as he has free rein to live out his life in us. Of course, Christ does not feel insecure, inadequate, guilty, or have worries, doubts, or fears. So those things are progressively expelled from the life. If they are gone from the life, then we are no longer a bundle of frustration. If we are not frustrated, then we are not hostile. When the outer stresses occur with Christ at the center, then we do not react with hostility; but Christ in us responds with just the opposite—love, understanding, and compassion. And then, of course, if there is no frustration and hostility to be kept bottled up inside, there is nothing to adversely affect the mind or emotions. The mental and emotional symptoms are purged from the life. And if all that has caused the conflict inside is gone, the resulting psychosomatic symptoms leave also.

DIAGRAM 6

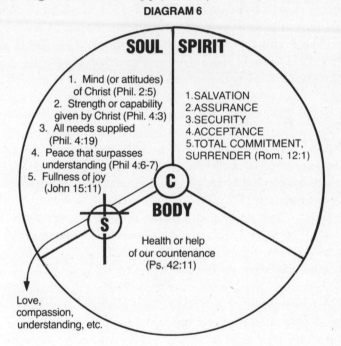

SOUL | **SPIRIT**

1. Mind (or attitudes) of Christ (Phil. 2:5)
2. Strength or capability given by Christ (Phil. 4:3)
3. All needs supplied (Phil. 4:19)
4. Peace that surpasses understanding (Phil 4:6-7)
5. Fullness of joy (John 15:11)

1. SALVATION
2. ASSURANCE
3. SECURITY
4. ACCEPTANCE
5. TOTAL COMMITMENT, SURRENDER (Rom. 12:1)

C

S

BODY

Health or help of our countenance (Ps. 42:11)

Love, compassion, understanding, etc.

Naturally, if the body has undergone organic damage, such as a duodenal ulcer, usually it takes time for that to heal. But many times we have seen instantaneous deliverance from such things as tension headaches, nervous stomach, and other pain caused by tension. When "the peace of God which passes all understanding" becomes the rule of life, then these things must go, whether the Holy Spirit does it gradually or more dramatically.

47

Now, the logical question is, How does Christ *become* the center of the life? What truth in God's Word explains this to us? In order to grasp this, it is necessary to think through another illustration, the *line diagram* (Diagram 7). The horizontal line with an arrowhead at both ends represents eternal life; and, of course, eternal life has neither beginning nor end. Only one Being has eternal life, and that is God. So, in reality, eternal life is Christ's life. At a point in time, and at an appointed time, he came to Earth and took on a human body as a baby, being virgin-born in Bethlehem. But the life that he lived in that body is the same life that he has always lived as God. He lived in a human body for about thirty-three years, and then he ended his earthly existence at the cross where he bore our sins. He died, was buried, and rose again. And then his life continued.

At a later point in time, each of us entered into a physical existence by a physical birth. But, when we are born, we are not in his life. Instead, we are in another existence represented by the line going through our parents, our grandparents, and their ancestors all the way back to Adam. That is where our existence really began—in Adam. The hash marks represent generations from our parents back to Adam. It is easy to see that we were in our parents before we were born, and they in their parents. Therefore, if our grandfather had never had children, neither would we! Being in Adam, whatever happened to him happened to us.

We were *in Adam* positionally when he sinned. This is what made us sinners from birth. Paul explained, "Wherefore, as by one man sin entered into the world, and death by sin; and so death passed upon all men, for that all have sinned" (Rom. 5:12). Therefore, being *in Adam* when he sinned, we sinned. When he died, we died. So we are all born spiritually dead (Eph. 2:1).

When we were born, it was only natural that we would commit sin. We were born with a sin nature, or old man or Adamic nature. Paul emphasized, "For all have sinned, and come short of the glory of God" (Rom. 3:23). We sinned, consistent with our nature, and our natural progress was downward. The diagram showing the life "in Adam" indicates this downward trend. This is verified by Paul's words, "For the wages of sin is death [spiritually and eternally as well as physically]; but the gift of God is eternal life through Jesus Christ our Lord" (Rom. 6:23). Since we are born spiritually dead, our greatest need is life. We received physical life by physical birth and we likewise receive spiritual life by spiritual birth (John 3:3; 1 John 5:11-12). The transition line depicts the truth propounded in 1 Corinthians 1:30: "But of him [God] are ye in Christ Jesus, who of God is made unto us wisdom, and righteousness, and sanctification, and redemption." We are taken out of the old Adam life and put into Christ by the Spirit of God. Once we are *in* Christ, we are in an eternal existence, a life that is not based on time.

We have asked this question of literally thousands of people: "What is eternal life?" Some reply, "It is life after death." Others may add, "I don't believe in it." When asked when it starts, they might reply, "When I die." Others may say that eternal life begins when they are saved, which is, likewise, incorrect. It didn't start when we were saved. Eternal life didn't start. It always was! The truth is that once we have entered into the life of the Lord Jesus Christ, we have entered into *eternal life,* a life that spans the past as well as the future.

This new life is traced back—not through our ancestors to Adam—but back through Christ to (and beyond) the cross. Calvary is an event in eternity. Being *in Christ* means being in him eternally. Our life in Christ is an eternal relationship. Eternity is always present tense since it is not based on time. This means, then, we were in him *at the cross.* We were in him not only when he was crucified, but when he was buried and when he was raised from the dead and when he ascended into heaven. This is an identification clearly established in Romans 6:4-6 and Colossians 3:1-3.

The same truth is further stated by Paul's assertion, "I am crucified with Christ" (Gal. 2:20). We could not be crucified with Christ unless we were in Christ. Paul wrote that we were not only planted or buried with him but *raised from the dead* with him (Rom. 6:5). Accepting Christ means that we are raised to a

DIAGRAM 7

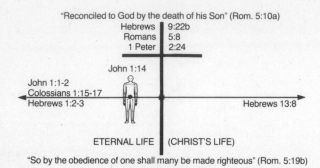

"Reconciled to God by the death of his Son" (Rom. 5:10a)

Hebrews	9:22b
Romans	5:8
1 Peter	2:24

John 1:14

John 1:1-2
Colossians 1:15-17
Hebrews 1:2-3

Hebrews 13:8

ETERNAL LIFE   (CHRIST'S LIFE)

"So by the obedience of one shall many be made righteous" (Rom. 5:19b)

heavenly level of life. Scripture shows we are seated right now at the right hand of God *in* Christ (Eph. 2:6).

Paul turned our perspective back in time: "He hath chosen us in him before the foundation of the world" (Eph. 1:4). Like most spiritual truths, this may be difficult for our finite minds to grasp; but this eternal relationship is just as much true in the past as in the future, since time is not an issue.

This, then, is the manner in which Christ becomes the center of our lives. We not only are to understand this truth intellectually and theologically, but also to enter into the experience of it by an act of faith. We are not referring to some experience where self or the flesh is permanently removed and we obtain sinless perfection; and we are not referring to what is sometimes termed a second work of grace. We are talking about entering into something experientially that is already ours positionally—the life of Christ. Though his life is a blessing received the day we were saved, we need to enter into the fullness of Christ, into the Spirit-filled life, into the abundant life or the abiding life, as the Bible variously terms it.

The difference it makes is that we cease trying to live for him and to work for him and to witness for him in the energy of the flesh. Discovering by revelation, or better, illumination, that we

DIAGRAM 8

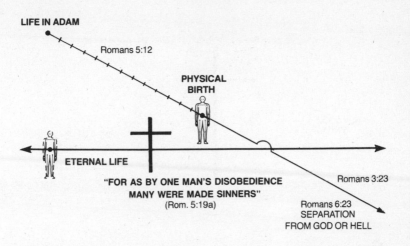

have been crucified and raised to new life, we can now reckon this to be so and let him live and labor through us. But this demands that we come to the end of ourselves and all our resources. "Not I, but Christ" is the way Paul expressed it (Gal. 2:20).

How can this awareness of "no longer I but Christ" take place? It happens differently in every life. But in point of time, it has to become as much a reality as the day we trusted Jesus Christ to save us. And it is, likewise, *by faith.* According to Scripture, we have to "reckon" or count this to be so. "Likewise reckon ye also yourselves to be dead indeed unto sin, but alive unto God through Jesus Christ our Lord" (Rom. 6:11).

Reckoning, or counting upon the fact of crucifixion and resurrection with Christ is an act of volitional choice or an invoking of the will to appropriate that which God's Word states to be true of us in Christ. This is an act or decision of faith identical in all respects to that of trusting Christ as Savior. God's Word states that we are sinners and that the Lord Jesus Christ fully finished the work for our redemption at Calvary; we claimed this by faith, in repentance and surrender, and were born again. In the same way, God's Word (the same source) indicates that we are "self-

51

ers" (controlled by the flesh) and that we participated in his death, burial, and resurrection, and ascension, thus freeing us from slavery to sin's power.

DIAGRAM 9

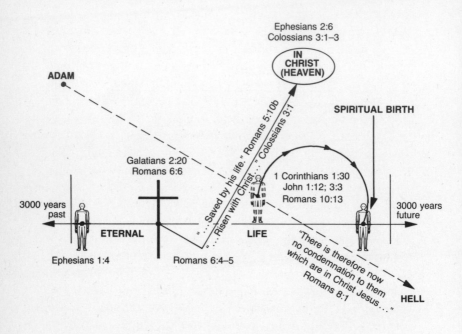

Again, by volitional choice, we appropriate Christ as our Life just as we appropriated Christ as our Savior. In response to our act of faith in appropriating Christ as Savior, the Holy Spirit regenerated us in our spirit; in response to our appropriation of Christ as our life, the Holy Spirit renews us in our minds (Rom. 12:2). The *will* is the vital function since the emotions may be at variance with the facts. As we choose against the world, the flesh, and the devil and count upon the indwelling Christ to be our life, we are choosing to have our minds renewed by the Holy Spirit. Consequently, our emotions are brought into congruence with truth (Eph. 5:18) so that we can "walk not after the flesh,

52

but after the Spirit" (Rom. 8:4) and abide in him (John 15:5).

In some, this has occurred in a gradual way. As they began to understand their position in Christ and his life in them, there was a dramatic transformation. Although this process was gradual, they *knew* that a new awareness of being in Christ had altered their attitudes in many ways.

We have also seen this identification-realization take the form of a dramatic and sometimes traumatic crisis as God began to make this a vital, living reality. The important thing is not how it takes place, but that we are certain it happened—that it is now no longer "I," but Christ living and reigning within. This process is described in greater detail in Chapter 5.

To reiterate, we must realize that this identification awareness is an event that actually takes place at a point in time and experience. We may not be able to identify that crisis point, the process may be so gradual. But the result is unmistakable—self is dethroned and Christ is enthroned. This, then, is the way we enter into the Spirit-filled or Spirit-controlled life; we enter in by the way of the cross through death and resurrection with Christ.

The reality of this does not have to take years and years after conversion. We may realize at the new birth that not only was he crucified *for* us but that we were crucified *with* him. It is all true, as far as God is concerned, the day we trust Jesus Christ.

At our counseling office, we sometimes admonish people after they receive Jesus Christ as Lord and Savior: "Don't you ever *try* to live the Christian life! You have invited the Lord Jesus Christ into your life—let him live his life in you. That's why he entered your life." It is a life that is lived by faith. And, when we understand this, we see that there is no way we can live a Christian life. It is not a set of rules that we keep. That is legalism. It is the law that gives sin its power and spurs many believers on to overt or covert rebellion.

Valiant attempts to restrain sin from without rather than allow the Spirit to constrain from within, often produce exactly the opposite results from those intended. Being enslaved by laws is not freedom (Gal. 5:1). "Ye shall know the truth," Jesus promised, "and the truth shall make you free" (John 8:32). This kind of freedom is inviting Jesus into the life and then letting him live his life in ours. However, it is not a life of passivity but of aggressively yielding our will to his working.

If we are to struggle to live *for* him, then he cannot live *through* us. Until self is dealt with, we continue the self-struggle, perhaps even asking him to help us. We may spend effort and money for him. But this isn't the Christ-centered life. It is simply trying to harness the self-life to work for God. During this time of trying, or this trying time, God uses us in spite of ourselves; but he cannot give us the Spirit-empowered ministry he wants us to have. He cannot multiply and master our ministry to the point where he is doing it through our yieldedness.

It is his goal, his purpose, that we should be conformed to his image (Rom. 8:29). If we are going to know this conformity, we have to be made "conformable to his death" (Phil. 3:10) and experience his cross. This is the only way that Christ can become our life initially, as well as perpetually. We must let him do the living, so that he can work unhindered through our lives. How this can become a reality is answered by the "Wheel of Life" chart.

Are you ready to stop spinning your wheel, so that Christ can become your center? Has God convicted you of the utter corruptness and sinfulness of the flesh? Unless and until we have seen this picture stand out in bold relief, we will not see the absolute necessity of denying ourselves and taking up the cross (Luke 9:23). If you are, just close your eyes, bow your head, and pray a *selfer's* prayer. Tell God that you surrender and that he can take over and do whatever he wants with you. Admit or confess that you have been attempting to live the Christian life in your own strength. Then claim by faith your death, burial, resurrection, and ascension with Christ and thank God for saving you from yourself, and trust him to live his life through you. "Yield yourself unto God as those that are alive from the dead, and your members as instruments of righteousness unto God" (Rom. 6:13). If the surrender is unconditional, the responsibility for directing the life and the spiritual maturation process has been given to God. The time and matter of consummation will differ in each life. God has promised, "Faithful is he that calleth you, who also will do it" (1 Thess. 5:24).

THREE
WHAT SPIRITUAL MATURITY REALLY MEANS

Spiritual growth or spiritual maturity are terms representing a very vague concept in the minds of most Christians. Many Christians define a "mature" Christian on the basis of the things he does *not* do, much as a psychologist describes a "normal" person by the absence of symptoms. In other words, a person who is conscientious in observing certain taboos, such as drinking and smoking, and who actively participates in the ministry of the church, is considered a "good" Christian.

Another common yardstick for measuring a person's spiritual growth is his prowess as a soul winner—introducing others to the Lord Jesus Christ. Of course, this does represent a degree of growth. And it is proof of new life, since we beget after our own kind. However, witnessing or soul winning can be done with self in control of the life, or as the Scripture says, "after the flesh." This is supported by the fact that many Christians have never experienced the cross and the reality of the Christ life as presented in the previous chapter. And yet, they are used by God in personal and corporate evangelism. While maturity is generally defined in terms of refraining from sinful activities and being involved in Christian service, frequently this has little or no spiritual significance in that there is relatively little permanent change in life-style.

DIAGRAM 10

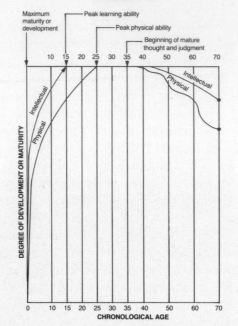

Many a Christian is in a sort of spiritual no-man's-land. He has no idea how to proceed in spiritual growth even though he may have the motivation. Since Spirituotherapy is basically counseling for spiritual growth, it is necessary to illustrate some guidelines that are valuable in objectively assessing progress in being "conformed to the image of Christ."

These charts (Diagrams 10 and 11) present some typical growth patterns in the lives of Christians and afford the possibility of comparison for the purpose of evaluating our spiritual lives. It is to be understood that the growth patterns are representative of what *is*. They are not ideal in any sense of the term. It is certainly not God's will that we should go for years or even a lifetime as a spiritual infant or adolescent. It is his desire that we go on to maturity. "Therefore let us leave the elementary teachings about Christ and go on to maturity" (Heb. 6:1, NIV).

For purposes of comparison, we have also added typical patterns for physical and intellectual maturity. The horizontal line at the base of the diagram represents our chronological age—our threescore and ten years that we may or may not be given. The vertical line at the left indicates relative growth or maturity. The upper horizontal line is indicative of the maximum maturity we attain in this life. Of course, this cannot be objectively quantified; and it is different for every person. For the purpose of clarity in verbally explaining the chart, it is necessary to assign numbers to each of the spiritual (or carnal, as the case may be) patterns.

We will begin on Diagram 10 with the path depicting the process of physical growth and decline. As represented by the "0," we are born and grow rather rapidly for the first few months. The birth weight should be doubled in about three months and tripled in six. Then the rate of growth declines, or else we would rapidly become giants. The peak of physical maturity is at about age twenty-five. After that, there is a gradual declension in physical vigor, along with the usual physical ailments, as the body begins to wear out. These are represented by the jogs in the right half of the line with the life terminating at age seventy. In other words, after age twenty-five, things are bound to get worse unless they have been terribly bad before that.

Our intellectual growth is even more rapid, with the peak in rate of learning being reached in the midteens. This remains fairly constant through our twenties and then begins to recede. As represented on the chart, we begin to attain more mature thought about age thirty-five since we have made enough mistakes that we should have profited by experience. As we get older, we *should* get wiser.

If we could chart emotional maturity, we would find that emotional symptoms stemming from youth are amplified as the body begins to lose its reserve of physical stamina. In our younger years, we have sufficient strength to maintain our "fronts" or defense mechanisms and continue to be somewhat productive in our various life roles. As our physical strength wanes, we are faced with the fact that there is insufficient brain and brawn to fight the battles on the inside and the outside. Our responsibilities may deter us from "copping out" on external activities, but we are increasingly ineffective in maintaining our facade, and the emotional symptoms we have had all along become more glaring. This is the reason we see so many in their forties yielding to a variety of neuroses and "nervous breakdowns." The symptoms can no longer be kept under wraps.

DIAGRAM 11

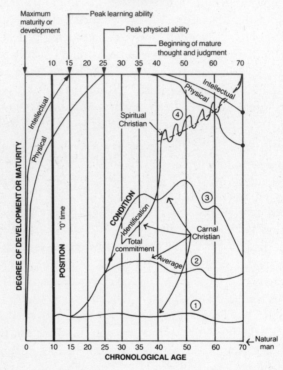

Now, let us concentrate on the several lines represented in the spiritual state of man. The bottom of the chart, the horizontal, depicts the "natural" man, or the man who has never been saved from his sinful state. There is, consequently, no change in his spiritual condition from birth. He is born estranged or separated from God and will remain so eternally, unless he comes to know eternal life in Christ.

The vertical line at age ten represents spiritual birth or regeneration—conversion. We have selected this as the average age at which a person enters into a personal relationship with the Lord Jesus Christ.

At this point, we must explain two other concepts—that of *position* and *condition*. These are often referred to as *standing* and *state*. It seems easier to distinguish between the two by using the former. Looking at the vertical dotted line from age ten, it continues upward until it intersects the maximum maturity line at the top of the diagram. This is to indicate that in "0" time— immediately and eternally—we are considered perfect or justified in God's view of us. This is our *position* as Christians. He sees us as dead to sin and the law (Rom. 8:2) and "alive unto God through Jesus Christ our Lord" (Rom. 6:11). Our position is perfect, since we have been given a standing *in* Jesus Christ (1 Cor. 1:30), and we are presently seated together "in heavenly places in Christ Jesus" (Eph. 2:6).

Though our spiritual *position* is perfect, our spiritual *condition* may be pathetic! The solid vertical line at age ten indicates some initial change in the life after conversion. But, since most ten-year-olds are not gross sinners, there is usually not a great transformation in the life at the time of salvation. Looking to the right at line number one, we see that there is little positive change in the *condition* as time passes. This line represents the person who does not receive sufficient spiritual food (1 Pet. 2:2) and goes through life suffering from spiritual malnutrition. Even though he has been brought to life through a spiritual birth, there is little discernible growth "to be conformed to the image of his Son" (Rom. 8:29). In fact, the day he dies he may be in a worse condition than the day he was saved because of the realization that he has wasted his entire life.

Line number two illustrates the average garden-variety Christian. There is a period of little or no growth for a number of years. Some growth begins during the teenage years. It continues as he (or it can just as well be she) takes on the responsibilities of parenthood, including taking the children to church. While the children are growing up, he is active in church and performs some service. God uses him to some extent during this period of time so he feels that he is a "good Christian." When the children leave home, he says to his wife, "Let's let the younger ones do it; we've done our part." He becomes inactive spiritually and begins to coast downhill.

After a number of months or years, he develops a twinge of conscience and decides to try again to be active. For a while the curve turns upward. There is an increase in activity and some growth, but it is still not satisfying so he goes down farther this time. Near the end, there is a spurt of effort and spirituality as he crams for his finals. This path represents more defeat than victory even though God honors the effort expended.

The other two lines, numbers three and four, represent Christians who have made a "total commitment" or have completely sold out to Jesus Christ. Line three describes the man who is concerned with his service for Christ. He is a regular beehive of activity. He may be an active (or hyperactive) layman or minister who is involved in Christian activity, morning, noon, and night. He is generous in his outlays of money as well as time, proving that he has a real burden for the souls of others.

After a good number of years, usually, his defeats begin to outnumber his victories, and he falls back and regroups. He loses ground for awhile and then changes churches or makes some other adjustment and charges ahead again, full force. He gets a little higher this time, and God may bless his service, but he has farther to fall and does so. He still has not recognized that most of his "accomplishments" are little more than sincere self-effort. So he gathers all his strength for one more gallant try. Failure this time results in the layman dropping out of church or the pastor leaving the ministry. God may bless and use someone who follows such a pattern, in spite of himself; but the person never goes on to spiritual adulthood. It is always some sweet victory along with much defeat. It is an experience-centered life rather than a life of steady growth.

The final path, line four, represents the believer who matures into spiritual adulthood. He, too, has yielded totally to the Lord Jesus Christ, but he is interested primarily in his growth rather than in his service—in *being* rather than *doing*. As a result, he doesn't come on quite as strong as number three, but he is probably used of the Lord as much or more. He goes along at a steady rate of growth for a number of years, and he also begins to have problems. He feels that everything is going backwards and that he is bringing reproach to the Lord's name. It may be physical problems, psychological symptoms, conflicts with children— these and many other things deplete a believer's self-resources and bring him to the end of himself. He is still going uphill but at a slower pace because he must come to utter helplessness. Only then is he ready for the cross. The chart spots this (the vertical line) at age forty because this is a conservative estimate of the average age at which a Christian enters into an abiding, abundant life of identification with Christ. This is not to say that a person can not appropriate the Christ-life earlier. It is merely a statement of fact about present-day Christianity, at least in the United States.

Primarily because of ignorance, identification usually does not become a practical experience for many until years after the life has been totally surrendered to the Lord Jesus Christ. God uses adverse circumstances along with enlightenment in his Word to bring us to the end of our resources. We get so sick of ourselves we cannot stand ourselves. Usually, only after we have reached this point does the truth of crucifixion with Christ and life in Christ produce a deep, dramatic transformation. Often the change is much greater than at salvation. When we are saved, the sin is forgiven; but the flesh continues to pump out the sins. As with Paul in Romans 7, we are doing the things we do not want to do and not doing the things we do want to do. After identification, it is the Lord Jesus living his life through the individual—a totally different quality of life.

The transformation may be gradual or sudden, but it is real in either case. Occasionally, there is a period of near euphoria because of the peace and freedom that is realized. This may last for hours or days. But, inevitably, self sneaks back into control as represented by the dip after the peak has been reached. Since the person is down, with self back in control, he is a prime target for satanic attack. Satan always hits us while we are down! In fact, this is the only time he can really get to us. The first attack is

63

usually hard on the heels of the identification realization. Being forewarned, we should be forearmed. The Word tells us that we should not be ignorant of Satan's devices (2 Cor. 2:11). Also, "Resist the devil and he will flee from you" (James 4:7).

When we revert to self-control, the remedy is the same as when victory was realized in the first place—to reckon or account ourselves to be dead to sin and alive to God (Rom. 6:11). It is not a one-time experience that insures constant victory, but it must be a "daily" or "always" reckoning upon our deliverance to the cross. Jesus declared, "If any man will come after me, let him deny himself and take up his cross daily and follow me" (Luke 9:23). Paul expressed the same idea: "For we which live are always delivered unto death for Jesus' sake, that the life also of Jesus might be made manifest in our mortal flesh" (2 Cor. 4:11). The cross spells death and deliverance as far as the reign of the flesh is concerned. We triumph always and only in Christ (2 Cor. 2:14).

After a new sense of freedom is experienced as a result of entering into identification, it is necessary that we have *assurance* of identification. This is parallel to and just as vital as being sure of salvation. Unless we have assurance of salvation, we will not possess our possessions in Christ. Unless we have assurance of identification, we cannot rest in the finished work of Christ. This is particularly important when we revert to self for the first time. Based on feelings, our inclination may be to conclude, "I lost it. *I* won't ever have that joy again. *I* didn't read enough. *I* didn't pray enough." I, I, I—self in control and indulging in self-pity.

If we are certain that identification is a reality, we can be assured that we will never lose our stage of growth. We can no more go back across Jordan (as will be explained in chapter 4) than we can go back across the Red Sea. After identification, however, the battles are more severe than before, *if* we try to fight them in our own strength. If we do not have assurance based on his Word and corroborated in our experience, we are very likely to think it wasn't real and that we were kidding ourselves all the while. Just as we acknowledged our sins and were forgiven after salvation, we are now to acknowledge *self* and be "delivered unto death for Jesus' sake" that we might be restored to victory.

The only place of triumph is in Christ, not in self: "Now thanks be unto God which always causeth us to triumph in Christ and maketh manifest the savor of his knowledge by us in every place" (2 Cor. 2:14).

So long as the Lord Jesus is in control, we will be up. When *we* are in control, we will be down. In the beginning, there may be a transferring of control back and forth from self to Christ until we learn how to exercise our wills in faith that he might more consistently live his life through us. This is a lifetime learning experience, but we gradually find it more supernaturally natural to permit him to retain control. The Word promises, "Being confident of this very thing, that he which hath begun a good work in you will perform it until the day of Jesus Christ."

Appropriation of the truth of our identification with Christ does not constitute maturity. It signifies, rather, our becoming spiritually adult. It is very similar to age twenty-one, physically, at which time we become legally adult. But there is much maturing that must take place afterward. The ups and downs are some of the growing pains of maturing spiritually.

Referring back to the curve showing the physical decline, we can now indicate some correlations. If we are maturing spiritually as we should, the physical decline is not fraught with nearly as many dangers from an emotional standpoint. As we lose physical strength, we can draw from the Lord according to our need. As we continue to draw from him, we can maintain our emotional stability while increasing in wisdom and favor with God and man. Conversely, when we are spiritual dwarfs and are continually harassed by the exigencies of life, our aging bodies are inadequate to cope with the emotional demands. This sets the stage for a neurotic break or a variety of escape mechanisms.

It should be pointed out again that there is no reason why it should be many years after salvation that we enter into spiritual adulthood. This is our birthright, and it can be possessed immediately upon experiencing salvation.

The ups and downs after identification are usually more violent in new Christians due to the lack of grounding in the basic principles of the Christian life. However, these new believers usually stabilize in a short period of time.

Which of the lines most nearly represents your life? Only as you are willing to be guided in an objective assessment or spiritual inventory by the Holy Spirit can you mature into a deeper and more wonderful relationship with our precious Lord. Don't stand still. Go on!

Abandon all rights to the helm of your life, and claim all that he is for all that you need, and he will make you what he intended you to be.

FOUR
WHEN LIFE IS LIKE A WILDERNESS

The previous chapter presents a method of graphically depicting spiritual growth that has proven effective in helping troubled Christians assess their spiritual condition or state. However, it was developed by man and must be accepted as such. In this chapter a similar purpose is intended, but a scriptural analogy is used for which there is more than sufficient warrant.

The journey of the children of Israel from Egypt into Canaan affords a comparison for the stages of spiritual growth in the Christian. The Old Testament book of Joshua furnishes some of the most valuable illustrations of defeat and victory, and the New Testament book of Hebrews offers striking comparisons. Hebrews refers to Israel as an "example of unbelief." The results of both belief and unbelief are carefully detailed.

God deals with us as individuals in a manner similar to the way he dealt with the children of Israel as a nation. As shown in Diagram 12, their progress was from Egypt through the Wilderness to Canaan. God promised the land of Canaan to the children of Israel while they were yet in Egypt, just as he promises us a victorious life (Canaan) when we accept his Son, the Lord Jesus Christ. Egypt was a place of slavery for the children of Israel for four hundred years, and it represents the slavery of sin into which each of us was born. The Red Sea was the means of deliverance from Pharaoh's army for the children of Israel. When God opened the sea, they escaped across on dry ground. In the analogy, the Red Sea is typical of our deliverance from sin and bondage through trusting the Lord Jesus Christ.

The Wilderness was a place of wandering for forty years. All the Hebrew men over age twenty who came out of Egypt, except two, died in the Wilderness because of unbelief and disobedience—including Moses, their leader. Joshua and Caleb were the two believing ones who took God at his Word and went on into Canaan. Similarly, relatively few Christians enter the place of victory typified by Canaan.

The Red Sea is a picture of salvation; the Jordan River is a picture of identification with the Lord Jesus Christ. The children of Israel did not enter in because of unbelief (Heb. 3:19), and many Christians follow their example. They feel that God ran fresh out of miracles the day they were saved. It certainly took a miracle to open the Red Sea, and it takes a miracle of grace to change the human heart at salvation. It also took a miracle to open the Jordan River, and it is a miracle of illumination when we see that we are crucified with Christ and are set free from our "Wilderness wanderings" to enjoy freedom and victory in the Lord—the victorious life is not a flowery bed of ease, but the battles are the Lord's, *if* we let him fight them.

In my opinion certain hymns and the theology they reflect have done a disservice to the spiritual growth of believers. Much of our theology can be shaped by the hymns we repeat so frequently. Thoughts such as, "I won't have to cross Jordan alone," and "I'm bound for the Promised Land" leave the impression that the Jordan is physical death and the Promised Land is heaven. This being the case, many Christians long for the victory of heaven while never expecting any victory in this present life.

Now we have the setting before us. We can begin to evaluate our spiritual growth in light of this journey. It makes us much less apprehensive about the trip when we know the destination and are instructed concerning the pitfalls along the way. True, we must still cover the terrain; but we can chart a course that is attended by the least difficulty *if* we believe our map.

DIAGRAM 12

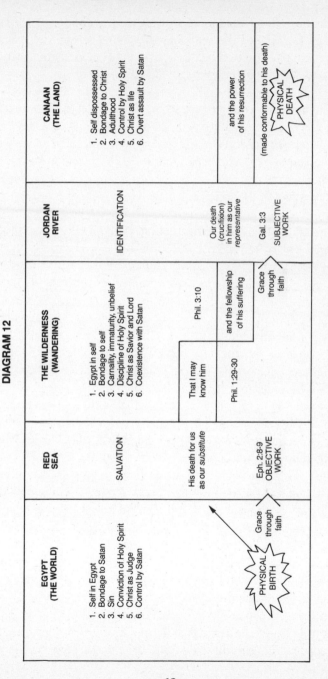

EGYPT (THE WORLD)	RED SEA	THE WILDERNESS (WANDERING)	JORDAN RIVER	CANAAN (THE LAND)
1. Self in Egypt 2. Bondage to Satan 3. Sin 4. Conviction of Holy Spirit 5. Christ as Judge 6. Control by Satan	SALVATION	1. Egypt in self 2. Bondage to self 3. Carnality, immaturity, unbelief 4. Discipline of Holy Spirit 5. Christ as Savior and Lord 6. Coexistence with Satan	IDENTIFICATION	1. Self dispossessed 2. Bondage to Christ 3. Adulthood 4. Control by Holy Spirit 5. Christ as life 6. Overt assault by Satan
	His death for us as our *substitute*	That I may know him — Phil. 3:10	Our death (crucifixion) in him as our *representative*	and the power of his resurrection
		and the fellowship of his suffering		
	Eph. 2:8-9 OBJECTIVE WORK	Phil. 1:29-30	Gal. 3:3 SUBJECTIVE WORK	

Grace through faith

PHYSICAL BIRTH

Grace through faith

(made conformable to his death)

PHYSICAL DEATH

In a journey across dangerous territory a map is indispensable if we are to reach our destination. When this diagram was once presented in a class, a man was overheard to say, "I wonder if I am closer to the Red Sea or to the Jordan." When this man saw a map of his spiritual journey, he was able to begin assessing his life. Not having realized that the Jordan was ahead, he probably thought that Canaan, or the victorious life, was heaven. As a result, he was unaware of the necessary preparation for crossing the Jordan, that is, experiencing the cross.

Many Christians are very bitter when this preparation by adverse circumstances begins because they are ignorant of the purpose. Their only recourse is to fight God rather than to cooperate with him and patiently endure "the fellowship of his suffering" (Phil. 3:10).

On a perilous journey we can be grateful for a map, but it is infinitely more comforting to have with us a guide who has made the trip before. Much of the apprehension is eased when the guide can prepare us in advance for the next segment of the journey and point out items of interest along the way. This is the purpose of the counselor in Spirituotherapy—to act as a spiritual guide. In this manner, the most direct routes can be taken and the stops and detours along the way can be explained.

Many times a person's suffering is not relieved immediately, but he can accept it more patiently when he understands the reason for it. Also, if he knows that immediately beyond that obstacle or trying circumstance is not only relief but deliverance, it is almost joy to endure the pain. Now, let us begin tracing the spiritual journey from Egypt to Canaan. Beginning at the left of the chart and proceeding to the right with each item, let us look at the progression as we consider various aspects of the Christian life.

First, when we are born, our entire being is in Egypt. This is the starting point for each of us. Then, when we are saved or cross the Red Sea, we find that some of Egypt is still in us. The children of Israel looked back across the Red Sea and remembered the leeks and garlic they had there and gave Moses a bad time because they had only manna to eat. And we continue in some of the same thoughts and behavior so typical of us before we trusted Christ. This is due to the fact that self is very much in the ascendancy. Once we cross the Jordan or experience the cross, self is dispossessed. Although the ground gained must be maintained by continuous reckoning, the stage of growth is never lost.

Second, the time in Egypt is a period of being in bondage to Satan, with him as our father and us as his slaves. After we have been Christians for some time, possibly many years, we begin to realize that we are in bondage to self. Paul described this vividly in Romans 7 in his admission, "The things I don't want to do, I am doing; the things I want to do, I am not doing." His internal turmoil brought him to the frustration he vented, "O wretched man that I am! Who shall deliver me from the body of this death?" (Rom. 7:24). He had seen self and its dominion in his life for the horrible thing that it was. It made him so sick he couldn't stand himself. That is great! Each of us must be brought to that realization if we are to be willing to submit to the suffering of the cross.

Until God turns on the searchlight of the Holy Spirit and illuminates his Word and our souls, we will not be "obedient unto death . . . of the cross" (Phil. 2:8). Once we have been dealt with in this manner, we are released from bondage to self to enjoy being bound to Christ, which is real freedom.

Third, our life during the time in Egypt is characterized by sin. We are born in sin, and we live in sin until its guilt has been dealt with by the blood of Christ.

Many Christians spend all their lives in the Wilderness, and some who eventually go on into Canaan have spent the majority of their lives wandering in the Wilderness. This is tragic but true.

The time in the Wilderness is a time of carnality, being controlled by self or the flesh. The word *carnal* in evangelical circles often denotes a Christian who is living in open scandalous sin. This may be the case, but a devoted minister who is working his heart out for the Lord and has never experienced the cross still has self in the ascendancy and is yet carnal, living and ministering in his own strength.

71

We might also label this as a period of immaturity—either spiritual infancy or spiritual adolescence. Assuming that we yielded to Christ as Savior and Lord at salvation and have continued to remain in a yielded condition, the length of time in the Wilderness is determined by God. We should not apologize for being a spiritual adolescent any more than we should be ashamed of being a teenager. So long as we are yielded to him, he takes us through the stages of growth and maturity in a time and manner commensurate with his intended use of the completed vessel. We can delay the process by an unyielded heart. It is the Holy Spirit's move if we stay yielded. Many times during the process, it is necessary for us to be subjected to adverse circumstances so that our surrender is renewed, thus demonstrating God's sovereignty.

Finally, it can be a period of unbelief and disobedience as it was with the children of Israel. They knew God had opened the Red Sea, but they didn't think he could open the Jordan. Many Christians forget that salvation is a miracle and do not expect God to continue his work of grace in their hearts. Therefore, they do not enter into the victorious or abundant life because of unbelief. Many do not even know that the Spirit-filled life is a live option for them. They seem to feel that it is only for a select few who are God's pets and that they are destined to live a life of defeat, failure, and frustration. Poor teaching of progressive sanctification can nurture this stalemate in spiritual growth.

This is the result of both ignorance and unbelief—sometimes fostered by the erroneous teaching that the Jordan is physical death and that Canaan is heaven. As a result, people are conditioned not to expect victory and peace here on earth. They are taught that they must be saved and that they are going to heaven when they die and that Christ may return at any moment. But in the meantime, it is just a mean time! The life of victory and power is for each of God's children. But resurrection power only follows crucifixion, and few seem willing to submit to its suffering. Even though our death in Christ is an accomplished fact at our new birth, the experiential realization of it usually comes through anxious times.

Fourth, the work of the Holy Spirit during the time in Egypt is to convict of sin. A thorough conviction of sin is essential before we will admit our need for the Savior. We must realize our sinfulness and lostness before we can be saved. After we trust the Lord Jesus, the work of the Holy Spirit is to discipline or teach us. Scripture uses the word *chasten* in this regard. The Scriptures say, "Now no chastening for the present seemeth to be joyous, but grievous: nevertheless afterward it yieldeth the peaceable fruit of righteousness unto them which are exercised thereby" (Heb. 12:11). When the discipline of the Holy Spirit has accomplished its purpose, we experience release from control by self and enjoy control by the Holy Spirit. This discipline could be looked upon as conviction of the flesh and as a parallel to the conviction of sin in the unbeliever. Such conviction is a necessary precursor to the cross. We cannot be filled or controlled by the Holy Spirit until self and its hold are broken. And this is only accomplished by the cross.

Fifth, during our stay in Egypt, Christ is our judge. We are at enmity with God and remain so until we have been reconciled through the blood of the Lord Jesus Christ. Paul wrote, "God commendeth his love toward us, in that, while we were yet sinners, Christ died for us" (Rom. 5:8). Once we receive him (John 1:12) we become sons and are no longer at enmity with him. During the Wilderness time he is our Savior, and when we yield totally to him, he also becomes our Lord. This is one of the most important decisions a Christian ever makes.

This unreserved yielding to him is "our reasonable service" (Rom. 12:1) and is prerequisite to our going beyond the Jordan and knowing the Lord Jesus as our very life. Paul said, "For to me to live is Christ" (Phil. 1:21). This must take place by the illumination of the Holy Spirit. We can understand it intellectually, but the life of Christ becomes real within us as he is revealed by the Holy Spirit. Paul testified that "it pleased God, who . . . called me by his grace, to reveal his Son in me" (Gal. 1:15-16). The Lord Jesus Christ is revealed *to* us at salvation, but he must be revealed *in* us. Paul wrote, "We are always delivered unto death for Jesus' sake, that the life also of Jesus might be made manifest in our mortal flesh" (2 Cor. 4:11). Others cannot see him in our lives until first he has removed *us* out of the way.

Paul stated it another way: "My little children, I travail in birth again until Christ be formed in you" (Gal. 4:19). He cannot be formed in us until he has first dealt with the ugly self that resists conformity to Christ. Both the need and the answer must come by revelation (illumination) of the Holy Spirit. He must increase and we must decrease. We decrease to nothing so he can be everything—our very life.

Sixth, we must consider the work of Satan during the three periods of time. The time in Egypt is a time of total control by Satan. We are his subjects since he is the ruler of this world, and we are shackled by the bonds of sin, even though we do not recognize it until the Holy Spirit begins to draw us to Christ. During the Wilderness period, we more or less coexist with Satan. He doesn't bother us very much because we are hardly worth his notice. Self is doing an excellent job of keeping things in a mess so he just sits back and says, "Go to it, Self!"

The time in Canaan is an entirely different matter. We are promoted to the front lines, and those in the front lines of a battle are likely to become targets. Here we can expect direct satanic assault in a myriad of ways—attacks on our thought life, hindrances in our work, discouragement, sleepless anxiety, demonic harassment—varied, frequent, and subtle manifestations of the evil one. He is not stronger than our Lord, and he is a defeated foe, but we must not be "ignorant of his devices" (2 Cor. 2:11). To be ignorant is to invite trouble, because he goes about "seeking whom he may devour" (1 Pet. 5:8).

It might do us well to take a look at the battles in Canaan so that we are not surprised nor dismayed by the strife to be found there. Once the children of Israel were in the land, they still had to possess it, and they found it inhabited by seven tribes. The first battle to be fought in the Land was the battle of Jericho. The siege of this walled city could have been a much greater battle than any that they had fought in the Wilderness if they had fought it with their own resources, depending only on God for a little help now and then along the way.

They did not approach it in that way—they followed God's directions explicitly and the walls fell down without any effort on their part as they made the final shout (Josh. 6:20). They were cautioned by God not to take any of the "accursed thing" but utterly to destroy everything. But there was Achan, who was unwilling to be obedient. He stole some valuables and hid them in his tent (Josh. 7:21). And the result? The next battle they fought was a different story—the army that went against Ai was defeated. They scurried back to camp to determine the cause of the defeat. God showed them Achan's disobedience and commanded that he and all his possessions be destroyed. In other words, self must be brought back to the cross that Christ might again be in control.

The next time they went into battle, God gave the victory as he promised (Josh. 8:1) because he was in control. God, not self, causes us to triumph (2 Cor. 2:14). Victory is always and only *his* work in and through us. Paul emphasizes that "we are more than conquerors through him that loved us" (Rom. 8:37).

Looking at the lower portion of the Wilderness section of the chart, there is the breakdown of the verse beginning with, "that I may know him" (Phil. 3:10). Of course, we come to know him at salvation and continue to learn about him as we live with him. The next portion of the verse has been deliberately taken out of the order in which it appears in the verse that it might fit in with the order of the experience of many believers. The "fellowship of his suffering" is our lot as we experience his cross. Upon total commitment, the processing so vital to our being forced to the cross is begun. After the work of the cross in our lives, we can experience "the power of his resurrection." Only as we are at the cross can his power be manifested—and we must daily be "made conformable to his death."

When he is in control, he can exercise his power and his glory. He will never share his glory with another (Isa. 48:11). All the power that God used in raising Christ from the dead is available in us (Eph. 1:19-20), which makes it imperative that "the excellency of the power be of him and not of us" (2 Cor. 4:7). God demonstrates his power as we yield to him so that we can't consume it or use it for the fulfillment of our own lusts. When we attempt to do this, he withdraws his power until we are again at the cross and he can manifest himself to his glory.

Some other comparisons and contrasts might be observed. At salvation—illustrated by the Red Sea—we realize his crucifixion *for* us and appropriate his blood shed for our sins. At identification—typified by the Jordan—we realize our crucifixion *in* him and appropriate the victory his cross provides. Salvation is more of an *objective* work—something that is done for us. Identification is more *subjective* in nature—something that is done in us. In salvation Christ is our substitute; in identification he is our representative.

We entered into salvation by grace through faith; we enter into identification in precisely the same manner. Our salvation in all its states is grace at the beginning, grace at the end, and grace all the way through. We are not worthy to be saved from sin; neither are we worthy to be saved from self. But God in his infinite mercy deigns to have fellowship with us as redeemed sinners and to fill us with his life, love, and power in order that he may be glorified. Then, just as Joshua and Caleb spied out the land and came back with the minority report, we also must share with those yet in the Wilderness that the land of Canaan is indeed the Promised Land, flowing with milk and honey. However, like the faithful two, we must be prepared for rebuff because few Christians are receptive to the command, "Be filled with the Spirit" (Eph. 5:18), especially when they learn that they must first be emptied at the cross.

It usually takes considerable time and study before we are sufficiently established in the new life to be able to share effectively with those who are yet in the Wilderness. It seems that it takes most of a year for a person to be well enough grounded to be able to share with another without offending him. It usually takes considerably longer than that to learn to lead a person to the Jordan and go through the suffering with him as he proceeds downward to the cross. The person himself must take this step of faith into the Jordan before the water parts, "For we which have believed do enter into rest" (Heb. 4:3). "There remaineth therefore a rest to the people of God. For he that is entered into his rest, he also hath ceased from his own works" (Heb. 4:9-10). "Come unto me, all ye that labor and are heavy laden, and I will give you rest" (Matt. 11:28). Persons who are prepared by the Holy Spirit and have a clear view of the despicability of the flesh, or self-life, and an equally clear view of its scriptural destiny, the cross, are now ready to pray the "selfer's" prayer. An unsaved person controlled by sin is a sinner; a Christian controlled by self (the flesh) is a *selfer* (to coin a new term).

The unsaved person must concur with the scriptural conclusion that he is lost in sin and that Christ died for him and rose again. The carnal Christian must agree that there is nothing worthwhile in the flesh, and the scriptural remedy is that he died with Christ and rose again victorious over the world, the flesh, and the devil.

The sinner trusts Christ as *Savior*. The "selfer" trusts Christ as *Life*. We are reconciled to God by the death of his Son, but we are saved (from ourselves) by his life (Rom. 5:10).

FIVE
INTELLECTUAL
UNDERSTANDING—
THEN WHAT?

You may be thinking that this all makes sense intellectually and theologically, but how does it become a reality in *my* life? No, this is not just more knowledge to add to your collection of useless facts. This is the life that God wants for *all* his children, and he has no favorites!

So often we think that this all sounds appropriate for choice saints such as the Apostle Paul, D. L. Moody, Hudson Taylor, and those special few. But it is for *us!* While it is not *attainable,* it is *obtainable.* When we experience the Lord Jesus Christ as our life, we haven't really "arrived," unless it be at the foot of the cross. The cross was a place of humiliation, suffering, shame, and loneliness for our Lord. It will be the same for us—we are certainly not better than he!

You may also be prone to feel that this sounds plausible for others, but that you are too far gone, or too worthless, for God to do such a miracle in your life. Well, here is good news for you. It is just such persons that God meets and sets free.

One lady came for counseling who had been diagnosed as paranoid schizophrenic and had spent time at a nationally-known clinic and seven years in private psychiatric treatment. When she was told point blank that God would completely deliver her from all of these symptoms, she looked the counselor straight in the eye and explained her total disbelief that such as thing was possible. Less than four months and ten interviews later, God met her in a crisis experience and made a major change in her life.

Many tormented souls who come feel, "It just can't possibly happen in *my* life." But God is faithful to his Word and his calling. He meets those who are willing to meet him. His promise is that he will draw near to us if we draw near to him (James 4:8). However, he doesn't promise to chase us down!

Some come for counseling who want their lives to continue pretty much as they are, but without the problems they present. They may want *reformation* but are not willing to submit to total *transformation*. To be honest with them, the counselor must advise them that it may be necessary for them to endure more suffering. As long as they are trying to bargain with God, they may as well forget it. When they are willing to drop their conditions and meet his, then they are candidates for victory and will probably continue in counseling until they are set free.

If we sincerely desire the peace and freedom that only God can give, we must be willing to commit ourselves first to the Lord and then to a concentrated study program. This is an integral part of the counseling process, as well. Since it is our meeting with God, not counselors, that is going to be our source of deliverance, we must spend time in his Word and in studying books about spiritual growth.

After the intellectual understanding of the freedom we must continue to study the Word to comprehend more clearly our position in Christ. As we do, and reckon or account it to be so, the Holy Spirit will make it real in our experience. As we stated earlier, it may be a gradual dawning or it may take some kind of crisis. Very possibly, it will be even more real and transforming than the day we trusted Christ. Ours is to study and look to him. His is to reveal the life of the Lord Jesus in us.

As we begin to reckon upon these truths and God begins to deal with us, the ensuing struggle takes many forms. Some of the dilemmas that are regularly experienced by those in the counseling process are described in the remainder of this chapter.

80

AFTER TOTAL COMMITMENT

Some people are led by sincere and well-meaning Christian counselors or pastors to believe that the Lordship of Christ or total commitment is the epitome of the Christian experience. At times, this is true because there are those who equate Lordship with the walk in the Spirit. There is no problem with this, so long as the terms are clearly defined. The essential ingredient is the experience of the cross. The question is, What is total commitment?

When a believer comes to our offices for counseling, he is shown that any further progress in his spiritual maturity and subsequent deliverance from enslaving emotional symptoms is contingent upon his *total surrender.* The emphasis is on the *total,* and it is not made easy because it is not easy! It means surrender with no reservations—not friends, family, profession, future, possessions, habits, sinful relationships, or life-style. Anything that we are or have or might be is included in such a complete surrender. If we are dead serious, we are going to be seriously dead! Our surrender is, basically, our permission for our Father to take us to the cross.

Consider the story of the hen and the hog who were discussing the poverty program and what possible part they might have in the alleviation of hunger and suffering. Each made several suggestions, with the hen coming up with the idea that the world needed ham and eggs. The hog said, "For you that would mean a *contribution.* For me, that would mean *total commitment!*"

It is well to remember that such a commitment is an act of the will. The emotions may cry out against it, but the mind knows on the basis of God's Word that there is no other way. So, by a definite act of the will we choose God's way for our lives, not having any advance knowledge as to what this may entail. But, knowing that his way is the best way, whatever it is, we yield to him and trust him to bring it about in our lives (Ps. 37:5).

It is necessary to point out that this surrender and identification are not always simultaneous. In cases where a Christian is at his wit's end and learns of his position in Christ and yields to God completely, the Holy Spirit reveals it to him and it becomes

81

real in his experience at once. This is the exception rather than the rule, however, in the average Christian's experience. The experienced counselor may see many clients surrender and appropriate Christ as life simultaneously, since he is dealing with a biased sample—those who are in dire need. Not everyone in the church is this dependent at the same point in time, or we would have a problem on our hands.

Generally, the condition of the counselee actually worsens after the inception of counseling and subsequent surrender. This is only logical, because God first has to take him through a reduction process where he is reduced to nothing so that Christ might be everything—his all in all. But, again, if a person knows why he is getting worse, he does not push the panic button. He realizes the progress to the cross is downward. Only when we understand the purpose of the suffering can we appreciate the "fellowship of his sufferings" (Phil. 3:10).

Many times total commitment takes place at salvation, which should always be the case, or shortly afterward. Then a person may go through many years of preparation for the cross. If he is totally yielded, the length of time it takes for him to experience the cross is determined by the sovereignty of God. We can delay his work in our lives by hardening ourselves against his chastening (Heb. 12:11).

We have seen several people who were saved and who understood their identification with Christ at the same time. This resulted in in-depth work by the Holy Spirit making the Christ-life instead of the self-life evident from the beginning. This is not to say that they were immediately mature.

One such person was a young man who had recently spent four months in a mental institution. He was taking strong tranquilizers and barely coping with life. He declared himself to be an agnostic, but said he was willing to consider God's answer to his needs. In the first interview he yielded to the claims of Christ and was warned not to attempt to live the Christian life in his own strength. Returning the following day, he expressed ideas about how *he* should live the new life. This was exactly what we had instructed him *not* to do. He was again shown that it must be the life of Christ lived out in him.

That night he was planning to attend a ball game. Usually a handful of tranquilizers was needed to enable him to remain in a crowd, due to his paranoia. On this night, however, he had left his apartment and forgotten his tranquilizers. Since he hadn't been without them since he left the mental institution, he started back to get them and then thought, "The Lord doesn't need tranquilizers!" So he went on to the game, tranquilized only by God's Spirit, and enjoyed the best time he had experienced in twenty years.

Another young man was on LSD, speed, mescaline, cocaine, and marijuana from time to time, and his appearance matched his habit. He was born again in the first interview and was set free from the drugs and his life-style as the Lord Jesus became his life. He was terminated after the second interview. A short time later, he began preparation for the ministry.

Assuming that we remain yielded to God's processing and shaping, the length of time depends upon the way he plans to use our lives to his glory. We cannot effectively share with those who suffer if we ourselves have never suffered (2 Cor. 1:3-4). Our suffering is a time of learning and training for future usefulness. It can be an occasion for drawing closer to the Lord as he shapes his vessel, much as a potter molds his clay. Too often, we are prone to question whether the stages of shaping are necessary as the Master Potter unerringly molds us more perfectly into the image of his Son.

Another very significant point to keep in mind relative to surrender is that even though it is total in scope, it must be carried out in practice, item by item. In other words, we have surrendered the whole package; but he must now deal with everything in the package. Therefore, we find that many times afterward, we are holding on to this or that. But he gently breaks our grip, unless we are stubborn. Then he must take stronger measures.

But he that called is faithful (1 Thess. 5:24). It is almost as if we are being literally carried to the cross, and we grasp for everything we pass on the way. In his sovereign love, he remembers our initial surrender and continues to bring his way to pass in our lives (Ps. 37:5). What comfort there is in this knowledge! Even though we resist him and think we have reneged on our commitment and missed his will for our lives, he is faithful to perform that which he has begun (Phil. 1:6).

MORBID INTROSPECTION

Many Christians, and those fitting the description of neurotic behavior, almost without exception spend much time in looking inward. They may be searching for sin or evaluating this or that behavior or trying to justify their existence. Those who feel exceedingly inferior and worthless may spend most of their time contemplating their hopeless plight. The result? The more they look inward, the more miserable they become, in spite of the fact that they may view their self-searching and self-condemnation as proof of their sincerity, or as a kind of punishment by which they get even with themselves. They may conclude that God surely will reward them for their futile attempts to probe and purge and somehow make themselves acceptable in his sight.

This searching process is not only interminable and depressing to the believer, it is repugnant to God. The psalmist highlighted the fact that it is God's job to do the searching: "Search me, O God, and know my heart; try me, and know my thoughts; And see if there be any wicked way in me, and lead me in the way everlasting" (Ps. 139:23-24). The psalmist is praying, "*you* search me; *you* know me; *you* try me." But all too many Christians by their actions are trying to do the searching themselves.

At best, our searching can only turn up garbage, and sorting garbage is a most depressing avocation. Too, if we could ever complete the interminable task, we would wind up with neatly sorted piles of garbage, but still be blind to the *source* of all the garbage—self. When God turns on the searchlight, he is much more interested in dealing with the source than with the results. And he is always ready to "forgive our sins and to cleanse us from all unrighteousness" (1 John 1:9). But it must grieve him to see us plagued by the same besetting sins year after year. He always abhors sin and desires to rid us of it by putting it under the *blood of Christ*. Self—the flesh—is also the object of his abhorrence, and he yearns to rid us of its control and dominion through the *cross of Christ*.

When an overly introspective person ceases or attempts to cease this useless and harmful indulgence of self, he usually feels guilty for falling down on God's job! He always fails at it because he is playing God. That is a sure way to fail.

SPIRITUAL VERTIGO

This is a malady that affects a great many Christians. The term is derived from a condition pilots sometimes encounter in which their senses tell them that their aircraft is in a totally different attitude from that indicated by their instruments. They may have been accustomed to flying by sight and by feel so instrument flying presents a new challenge—they must fly by faith rather than by sight. They must have complete confidence in their instruments to the point that this faith will override their feelings.

Sometimes, a pilot's feelings tell him that his plane is level when he is really flying with one wing down on take-off or landing. Or he may suddenly be seized with the feeling that he is upside down. What does he believe—his feelings or his instruments? Of course, he must believe his instruments. He must act on the facts, which are more reliable than his feelings.

As Christians we are often faced with the same dilemma. If we are well adjusted psychologically, there is not as much disparity between our feelings and the facts. However, a person who *feels* inferior, insecure, inadequate, and unacceptable is continuously faced with a set of emotions that are at variance with the facts or reality. Therefore, he must distort the facts to agree with his feelings (commonly known as a neurosis) or employ some defense mechanism to permit him to cope with an untenable situation. Someone has said that the neurotic builds castles in the air, the psychotic lives in them, and the psychiatrist collects the rent!

A person may *feel* inferior when he really isn't. In fact, most who have extreme inferiority feelings excel in many areas. Because they *feel* inferior, there are many things they will not attempt, or they withdraw from certain situations—not because they cannot perform but because they *feel* they cannot. Naturally, this causes much frustration and internal conflict, and it is compounded because with their mind they *know* they can perform, but their emotions cry out, "No!"

It goes without saying that we cannot change our emotions, but *in Christ* we are not called upon to change our emotions. This also is God's job, and if we try to do it, it is just so much more futile self-effort. When we experience the Lord Jesus Christ as our life, he changes our emotions as a result of the renewing of our minds. All of these changes do not occur instantaneously. The transformation is effected by the Holy Spirit as we begin to place all of our confidence in "the instruments," the infallible Word of God. With our mind we must realize that God's promises are true and then determine with our will to act upon them. God will honor his Word and keep his promises to us, even if we *feel* that they are untrue or that he won't keep them (2 Tim. 2:13). As we consistently *will* to place our confidence in our infallible "instruments," the Word of God, our feelings will increasingly come in line with the facts. When this happens we no longer fit the label of neurotic, and our feelings are consistent with our faith in the facts.

SPIRITUAL SURGERY

Paul said that in Christ we are circumcised with the circumcision made without hands in putting off the body of the sins of the flesh—the flesh or self-life (Col. 2:11). In Romans, Paul wrote, "O wretched man that I am! Who shall deliver me from the body of this death?" (Rom. 7:24). Then he proclaimed that the victory is "through Jesus Christ our Lord."

Here we find the identification truths, the experiential removal of self as the master of the life—much like physical surgery. The analogy has many similarities.

Before physical surgery, there is generally, though not always, a period of time during which a person suffers from certain symptoms. This suffering convinces him that he has a need. These symptoms may plague one in various forms for several years before he sees a physician or before the surgery actually takes place. Often, he will try several remedies to suppress the symptoms in a vain effort to avoid surgery. When the adverse effects on the life are severe enough and the pain no longer tolerable, he realizes that something must be done.

Christians also try everything from hedonistic pursuits to compulsive Christian service. Or they may hit the tranquilizer bottle or seek spiritual "experiences" of various kinds. Anything is tried in order to avoid the spiritual surgery that must take place if they are to be set free and to be unhindered in their service for the Lord. It is similar to patients who try all the remedies and escapes until surgery becomes unavoidable. Even after it is known that surgery is the only way out, most persons postpone it as long as possible.

Once the diagnosis is made, it gives some relief if the patient knows that it is not terminal. There will be pain involved, but his life again will be normal after convalescence. Understanding the suffering removes the mystery even though the pain persists. The problem can now be dealt with realistically. We understand that whatever the adverse circumstances we are experiencing, it is permitted of God to point up the necessity of spiritual surgery. God does not allow this for punishment but for discipline or chastening so that our lives may be more free and joyful than before (Heb. 12:11).

Once all the escapes are blocked off, we must endure the surgery. As preparations are made for the operation, the patient must be rendered helpless. You can imagine how ludicrous it would be for the patient to jump around on the table in an attempt to "help" the surgeon. If the patient stirs, more anesthesia is administered. The surgeon neither wants nor needs the patient's help.

In similar manner, as God prepares us for spiritual surgery, he must take us through the process of defeat, failure, and suffering to render us helpless so he can do his work. Usually, we have done so much to "help" him, we want to continue doing so as he begins the process (Rom. 6:11). The surgeon of the body uses the scalpel. The Surgeon of the soul applies the cross to the source of the problem—*self.*

The divine Surgeon's purpose is not merely to take away the pain and restore us to our former way of life, in which self has dominated, but to enable us to enjoy the reign of the Christ-life instead of the self-life. Sometimes the surgery is short, and sometimes it is lengthy, depending on the nature of the case. In other words, the spiritual surgery may take place gradually, or it may be a crisis experience. In either event the result is the same—a transformation (Rom. 12:2) of the life by the renewing of the mind.

Then there is always the convalescence after surgery. This is rarely a smooth, uphill process. There are normally many ups and downs as we adjust to the new life. We may often revert to the old life with its defeats and frustrations—only to require a repeat of the surgery of the cross (Luke 9:23; 2 Cor. 4:11).

Finally, as in physical surgery, we delight to tell others of our successful surgery, and we are more than delighted to recommend the eminent and only Surgeon so that our friends may also know the joy and the rest found in the new life—the Christ-life.

SUFFERING IN PERSPECTIVE

Meaningless suffering is agony in the extreme. The physical pain may not in itself be unbearable, but the mental anguish becomes a cruel taskmaster. When misunderstood, suffering causes despair, defeat, and frustration. Often it is accompanied by resentment, bitterness, hostility, and depression. If, however, we can apply God's lenses to our eyes and see the goal he has in view, then we are afforded an entirely new perspective on the suffering. We may have endured untold suffering for years. But, when we come to appreciate it as the "fellowship of his sufferings," we recognize in retrospect that suffering is indeed a privilege (Phil. 1:29).

One lady came for counseling who, like the woman in Mark 5:26, had "suffered many things of many physicians." She recited her story about fifteen years with psychologists and psychiatrists, Christian and secular, in addition to the rounds of ministers and counselors. By that time she was almost nonfunctional. The counselor's comment on her condition was simply, "Wonderful!" Her look was one of amazement, not amusement. But, as she was shown the necessity of coming to the end of self, she began to see that empathy, not sympathy, was what she really needed. Years of such treatment had merely served the purpose of driving her farther down.

God used these circumstances to force her to the end of self. Realizing the reason for her suffering, she quit fighting God and trusted him to continue it until he had accomplished his purpose. She cooperated with him as he rapidly took her to the cross. In a very short time, she was released from the so-called mental illness for which she had endured years of symptomatic treatment.

THE DEATH BLOW

Suffering takes place over a period of time as the cross does its work. Yet, there must come the time when self yields completely to the cross. There are many signs of the end's approach. Usually, there is a period of deep anxiety just prior to the end. As in physical death, sometimes there is sudden "death" without a struggle. In other cases, there are the death throes as life leaves the body. Even though a patient may be dying of cancer and actually yearns to die because of the excruciating pain, as he begins to die, he instinctively tries to hold on to life. Similarly, even though a believer realizes that he is being drawn to the cross, it is almost as if the Lord has to drag him all the way, as he reaches for everything he passes.

If we have presented our bodies as "a living sacrifice" (Rom. 12:1), he is not going to heed our pleas for comfort until the sacrifice is consummated. The Father had to refuse to ease the awful agony of his Son on the cross as he cried out, "My God, my God, why hast thou forsaken me?" Just so, he cannot—he *must not*—ease the burden until his gracious work is finished in our experience. The Lord Jesus had no respite from his sufferings until he died. It was only after the suffering that Jesus entered the resurrection life.

We can be done a disservice by those who would relieve our symptomatic pain through ill-advised counseling. This is similar to offering relief to someone who is actually being crucified. If he were taken down, patched up, and given food, water, and blood transfusions, and put back on the cross, he could be kept alive for an extended period of time. If he has to die, however, he is not being done a favor by prolonging his suffering.

In our spiritual journey, the suffering of the crucifixion precedes the power of the resurrection. Paul gave the assurance that, "If we suffer, we shall also reign with him" (2 Tim. 2:11). We cannot bypass the cross and still know its power, nor can we experience the cross without its suffering. The theology of the cross cannot substitute for the experience of the cross in our lives. It is much more romantic to read about the trials and tribulations of great saints as God prepared them for ministry than it is to experience this ourselves.

Even though the atonement for sin was vicarious in that Christ shed his blood for our sins and, in so doing, gave us his life, his cross must become the *experienced cross* before his victory and power can be ours. In other words, we must enter into his life before we can share his death. Or to say it another way, it is through entrance into his life that we become partakers of his death. As the corn of wheat must fall into the ground and die to produce fruit, so also must we enter into his death before his life can be manifest in us in the bearing of much fruit (John 12:24;

15:5). "Whosoever will save his life must lose it" (Luke 9:24).

As we approach the cross, we must be brought to the utter end of our own resources. In doing so there are times when we think we cannot go on—that God doesn't love us or he wouldn't let us go through these difficult times. Or, we may suspect that our unsaved or saved mate is bringing all of this on us, or that it is the result of our sin (and it may be). We may even conclude that God delights in punishing us—perhaps because we do not have enough faith. All of these thoughts and many others may surge through our minds as we near the end of self.

Many times we try to "rescue" ourselves from this because we dread the pain or the humiliation. One by one, God eliminates the avenues that offer some temporary relief. When we fear that there is no way out but death, we have arrived at the truth. There isn't!

However, suicide isn't the answer because the problem is not confined to the body. It has invaded the soul. Suicidal feelings are not at all uncommon during this period of time since we feel that our faith is so weak that even God could not possibly do anything in our lives. In his grace, he made a way that we can get rid of ourselves and yet stay here—the cross.

We have been brainwashed to think that we must have greater and greater faith if God is to accomplish anything in and through our lives. In practice, however, we find that our faith progressively becomes weaker and weaker. Occasionally, the physical strength is also diminished to the place where a person is all but immobilized. This is something necessary so that he can get us out of his way until he can complete the work. One woman expressed it this way, "I'm so weak I can't even *help* God!"

Another woman in this situation discovered that she could not get out of bed one morning. Her husband notified our office that he would have to call in a psychiatrist. After additional conversation he agreed to bring her to the office. She limped into the counseling room and slumped into a chair. Only with great effort could she converse. When she was asked if she knew what was happening, she replied, "I think he is finishing the work." The counselor agreed. Then she said very slowly, "I'm just afraid I will get in his way as I have in the past, and he will not complete the work."

"You don't have to worry about that," she was assured. "He isn't even going to give you enough strength to get in his way!" She thought about that for a moment and then replied with measured words, "That's the happiest sad thought I ever had!" The counselor then shared this verse with her: "Even when we are too weak to have any faith left, he remains faithful to us and will help us, for he cannot disown us who are part of himself, and he will always carry out his promises to us" (2 Tim. 2:13, TLB). She received no strength until a day or so later when he set her free. His strength was made perfect in her weakness (2 Cor. 12:9).

THE NEW LIFE

When the process of this crucifixion experience is consummated, the result is spiritual resurrection life. Though it may be a gradual or a crisis revelation, the transformed life with its freedom is the proof that the Christ-life has become a reality. The manifestation of his life is different in each person. It usually takes several months for a person to become reacquainted with himself and to have some idea of what to expect by way of reaction to various circumstances. Many have made the statement, "I just do not know myself anymore." The reaction is much the same on the part of family members. Some spouses experience a state of mild shock as a result of being conditioned by past experience to expect unchanged behavior.

Although the stage of growth is never lost, the victory or joy of it may be, as self returns to the ascendancy in the life. It is most difficult not to return to past patterns of behavior and "try to live the Christian life." It is well to memorize and claim Galatians 2:20. Then, at the beginning of each day we can reckon ourselves, again and consistently, to be dead to sin, and trust the Lord Jesus Christ to express his life. The will must be engaged at all times. We *will* and he empowers (Phil. 1:6).

During the day we do well to remind ourselves several times, "It is not I, but Christ" and to expect that he will govern our plans and actions. We are not to become introspective and test every thought and action to see if Christ is responsible or self or Satan. We are merely to commit the day and our life to him and trust him to control us and each situation to his glory. Committing, trusting, reckoning—all are terms indicative of a functional will.

It is well to realize that if we regress to self in control, the defeats we suffer may be valuable learning experiences if we are determined to see them as such and not panic at our loss of victory and the hurt to self.

Many experience more "down" time than "up" during the early weeks of the deepened relationship as they gain discernment concerning the reassertion of self and the attacks of the adversary that are certain to come.

The excitement of life under Christ's control makes each day a new adventure when we are at rest and trust him who is our life to cause "all things to work together for good" (Rom. 8:28).

CHECKUP TIME

A diagram, similar to the one shown in chapter 3, has been meaningful in my attempts to explain some of these concepts. It is similar, but a bit less cluttered and more easily applied to life. While it is important to understand the psychological and interpersonal conflict that might be troubling us, it is much more important to get behind them and deal with the real issue—the identity out of which we are living that tends to perpetuate the self-defeating thoughts, feelings, and behaviors.

The chart might be used to help someone diagram his own testimony, to make a spiritual map that depicts the road over which he has traveled, and perhaps to gain a preview of what may lie ahead. But even a perfect map would do us little good if we do not know where we are.

Some years ago my wife and I were in Kansas City with some of our relatives. It was dark, and we became lost. We pulled over to the curb and spread the map out on the hood of the car under a street light to study it. We had a good map of the city and a car with plenty of fuel and in excellent running condition. But the map was useless unless we could find out where we were on the map. What we needed was someone to put an X on the map and say, "You are here."

The same is true of our spiritual "road map." We must know where we are if we are to know where we are going. We may be looking ahead for something that is already behind us. One woman, for example, had been immobilized with depression, despite many sessions with psychiatrists. Some years later, and before I met her, she attended a conference at which God transformed her life. For several weeks, she experienced victory that neither she nor her husband could believe. However, without a spiritual foundation she soon lost the victory and reverted to her old behavior patterns. Since she wasn't sure what she had lost, she didn't know how to regain it.

Later, she shared her story with me, and I was convinced that she had experienced the exchanged life but had no instruction as to how to continue her walk in the Spirit. Putting it in terms of Chapter 1, she had relinquished her "baby" but had never owned it. During the course of counseling, she was able to appropriate with knowledge what God had done for her and learned how to continue in victory.

Another way to consider this diagram is to think of how we would give our testimony about the significant mileposts along our spiritual journey. Most of us will have little trouble understanding the first milepost marked "Salvation," since many messages are preached on that vital subject. Also, it isn't too difficult to understand (though often difficult to do) what it means to make a "total surrender" of the life, the second milepost.

However, the third, "Identification" or "the Exchanged Life" may not be so easily understood. Suppose, for instance, that your pastor asked you to give your testimony at a Bible study he was holding. You might reply, "Sure, I am always ready to testify for my Lord." But the pastor goes on to give a stipulation regarding the content of the testimony. He asks you to omit all reference to the time when you were born again, because those in the class are already believers. He then says, "I would like for you to share with the class how God brought you to the utter end of yourself and what kind of mess you were when you got there. Then tell them how the cross of Christ became a reality, whether gradually or suddenly, and what the resulting transformation was like. Further, if I asked your parents, spouse, children, and friends to corroborate that testimony, could they?" In other words, the pastor was asking for a "before and after" testimony. What would be the response?

While such a testimony is not absolutely necessary for the cross of Christ to have become a reality in our lives, it is helpful in sharing with others if we are able to retrace our own steps to and through the cross. The diagram will not fit anyone precisely, but it may give us some idea of how we might portray what God has done in our lives, at least at the three basic junctures of "Salvation," "Total Surrender," and "Identification."

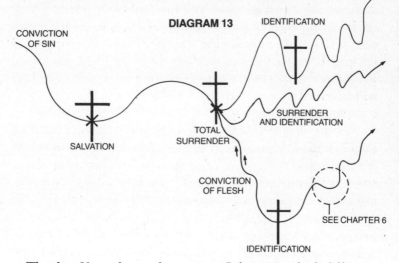

The first X on the road map is at Salvation, which follows a period of conviction of sin, when the Holy Spirit is drawing you to Christ. At this point you should ask yourself, "Have I truly been born of the Spirit?" Unless that has occurred, you should settle this matter with the Lord before going on.

If you are able to put an X there, what has been your life experience since that time? Were there changes that reflected your new life, and how long did they last? Did you at the time understand the ramifications of a total surrender to Christ as Lord, or was there another time when you took your hands off your life totally?

I asked an engineer, who had been a believer for a number of years, this question and he replied, "I will have to walk around the block a few times before I can do that." He walked around the block about six months before he returned. But, when he did, he was ready to do business with the Lord.

If you have reached the point of "Total Surrender" to the Lord, you can put the X at that point on the map. At that point on the chart, three paths are open. It would be preferable to take the center path, to appropriate by faith the blessings that come from "Identification" with Christ. Many believers enter into victory simultaneously with surrender in the counseling setting, since they are taught at that time about the experienced cross. This is because many who come for counseling are in desperate straits, which make them prime candidates for the crisis intervention of the Holy Spirit. Therefore, average Christians might take longer to appropriate victory since many of them aren't forced to look for immediate answers to critical problems.

Our total surrender is somewhat like the Lord's experience in the Garden of Gethsemane, where he said, "Not my will but thine be done." His surrender was valid, but it was several hours before he actually endured the cross. Our "Total Surrender" could be termed our personal Gethsemane—our permission granted to the Holy Spirit to make the cross a reality in our experience.

It may be, however, that your surrender to the Lord was not accompanied by an entry into victory but resulted in an attempt to try harder to make the flesh serve God. This would be represented on the chart as the uppermost pattern, which leads to frustration and defeat. Self-effort doesn't work much better after surrender than before. Coming to the end of self is never easy and is frequently painful. But it is extremely profitable if you learn the lesson that the Holy Spirit has patiently tried to teach you. If you can give testimony of having gone to the cross in your experience in a similar manner to this, place an X at the cross on the upper pattern.

Or, it may be that you surrendered some time in the past only to find things got worse. You may be following the lower pattern and are about to go even lower. This is, perhaps, the more common pattern in the lives of believers since most seem to grope their way through life by trial and error. When the pain increases, as depicted by the ups and downs, the flesh tries to calm the rough waters. The arrows pointing back to the place from which we came indicate our effort to try to do more of whatever brought us relief, however fleeting, in the past. Just as with using drugs and alcohol, it takes more and more activity to tone down the insatiable demands of the flesh.

Of course, all the things we do to alleviate the pain are couched in terms of self-effort, which is our basic problem in the first place. Such efforts are doomed to fail, but since we don't yet realize that reckoning ourselves dead to sin is the only way out, we do all *we* can do to avoid the cross. One of the first and most common things we do is to try to find victory through zealous applications of the disciplines of the Christian life. Now there is, of course, nothing wrong with Bible study, Scripture memory, prayer, regular church attendance, and church work. But such efforts accomplish little for us if we are trying to find victory through *trying* instead of *dying*. Therefore, as needful as these disciplines are, God won't honor our attempts to strengthen the flesh.

Many have discovered how futile it is to seek victory through their own efforts, even in the church, and have turned to other avenues to find meaning or relief from their inner turmoil. Many seek relief in some of the self-help programs that can be found in the world or in some Christianized editions at the nearest Christian bookstore. There is no doubt that some of these work, at least for a while. They are exactly what they claim to be—self-help, an attempt to increase the confidence in the flesh.

When the self-help programs don't work, some believers turn

to overt sin—to drinking, immorality, or other sinful pleasures. Of course, these only make the problem worse as guilt is added to whatever turmoil they had in the first place.

When a person has exhausted all that he knows that the church teaches, the self-improvement programs, and possibly some rebellion, he may turn to some kind of counseling or therapy. Of course, he or she would want to choose a Christian therapist that he might not be given advice counter to his beliefs. As we can see in the diagram, God has us programmed to go to the bottom—to the end of our resources—that we might deny ourselves and take up the cross. If the Christian is in therapy, rather than Christ-centered and cross-centered counseling, the therapist will unwittingly be saying, in effect, "Not if I can help it, you won't." And by his impeding the downward progress through alleviating the symptoms only, the suffering believer has been done a disservice. He is now stronger and can handle things better by himself. The *symptoms* may be better but the *problem* is worse. Now, it may take more adversity next time to bring him to the end of his fleshly resources. This doesn't mean that his therapist was intentionally sabotaging the believer's progress. However, if the therapist has not been to the cross in this sense, it is obvious that he would not practice an approach that leads others to the cross. The downward progress can be summarized under the rubric of "conviction of the flesh." Only as we see the flesh for what it is will we see the absolute necessity for the cross to become a reality.

What about it? Can you put an X at the cross, or are you still on your downward trek? It can be a relief to know why you are where you are. At least, you know where to go from there and that you can't do it by self-effort. The giving up and letting go can take some courage, since you are denying yourself the right to fix yourself.

As you place the X on your spiritual road map, remember that waiting passively for the next signpost to appear will all but guarantee a major delay in your spiritual growth. Just as in driving a car, the signposts come up as you move along—not while you are standing still. Faith is the dynamic that fuels the movement.

It is by grace through faith that we are saved from sin, and it is also by grace through faith that we are saved from ourselves.

As we get to the point of appropriation, emotions may play a major part in resisting our ability to lay hold of our victory in Christ by faith. Many have not discerned the difference between the activity of their minds and emotions. If there is emotional damage, the emotions may be totally unreliable. In this case, it is necessary to take action by faith, an act of the will, on what is known to be truth from the Word of God.

It is possible, then, to bypass damaged emotions and experience a renewing of the mind, which will in time result in the healing of emotions. What you *know* will eventually change the way you *feel.*

Suppose that you are driving down the interstate in your new sports car and you decide to see how it feels to drive considerably above the speed limit. So, you set it up to 120 miles per hour and cruise along while listening to your stereo, and everything seems wonderful. However, in the rear view mirror you see a car with a red blinking light. What you know (mental) causes some peculiar feelings (emotional), and in a split second, there is a sensation in the stomach (physical). Without too much prompting from the car behind, you begin to slow down to 100 and 80 and 60 and are preparing to pull off the road. But just at that moment, the policeman receives a radio call telling him of an accident up ahead, so he accelerates and leaves you in order to go to the accident. Now, does your internal situation reverse itself just as quickly as the onset of the symptoms? Or does it take a while for all the feelings to subside? More than likely, you can answer this from the crucible of your own experience. What you knew about the police car affected the way you felt almost instantaneously. But when you realize you escaped getting a ticket, the symptoms gradually dissipate. What you know will change the way you feel, but not always immediately. It is just so in our emotional makeup. Feelings that have been in place for a lifetime will respond to the renewing of the mind, but we must allow time for the process to take effect.

As you consider where you are in your spiritual journey, has the

99

Holy Spirit shown you what you are holding on to that is imped-ing your downward progress? It could be that there is some pet sin, a relationship, an old fear, the fear of freedom, an inadequate concept of God, a possession, fear of failure, or the loss of con-trol—any or all of these can thwart our progress and cause us to be defeated.

If God is to take control, we must lose control. And, so long as we are in control, we are really out of control. The willingness to lose control of all our circumstances is prerequisite to our finding our identity in the Lord Jesus Christ. Someone has aptly said, "We never know that he is all we need until he is all we have." The fear of losing control, even though what we are doing is not working, is probably the greatest fear that any of us faces. The prospect of losing the familiar, even though painful, for that which is unknown can be a frightening prospect.

Loss of identity can be totally demoralizing, depressing, and can even result in psychotic episodes. Some years ago, I was called to counsel with a young man in a distant state who had become psychotic. He had been hospitalized because he was out of touch with reality and was on massive doses of tranquilizers. He had planned to be a physician, but he had failed his examina-tion to enter medical school. His entire identity was wrapped up in what he was to become, and when that was denied him, he could not handle it and broke with reality. Underlying identity problems brought on his mental symptoms.

In a similar situation, I saw a young man once who had been a high school basketball star and had won a full scholarship at a major university. All was well until he damaged his knee in the closing game of his high school career. He ended up in a psychiat-ric ward of a hospital. Even though he was handsome, he was convinced that his face was grotesque. Since he had lost every-thing that meant anything to him—his identity based on basket-ball—he was unable to tolerate it and broke with reality.

A businessman had spent most of his waking hours in building several businesses. A series of events caused him to go bankrupt, and the consequent loss of identity caused him to wind up in a mental institution.

Losing identity with nothing to replace it can cause massive damage to the self concept and few can tolerate it. However, God does not ask us just to lose our identity but to exchange it for one that will work both for time and eternity. Whatever we have seen as our life must be given up if we are to know Christ as our life. We must lose our life in order to save it. Jesus said:

> Except a corn of wheat fall into the ground and die, it abideth alone: but if it die, it bringeth forth much fruit. He that loveth his life shall lose it; and he that hateth his life in this world shall keep it unto life eternal. (John 12:24-25)

A parallel passage reads, "For whosoever will save his life shall lose it; and whosoever will lose his life for my sake will find it" (Matt. 16:25). I do not believe it is doing violence to Scripture to substitute the word *identity* for *life* and make the passage read: "For whoever will save his identity shall lose it: and whosoever will lose his identity for my sake will find it."

Laying down our lives is not really optional—it is a command. "Likewise, reckon ye also yourselves to be dead indeed unto sin, but alive unto God through Jesus Christ our Lord" (Rom. 6:11).

The missionary martyr, Jim Elliot, caught the meaning of this when he wrote in his diary, "He is no fool who gives up that which he cannot keep to gain that which he cannot lose."

The ups and downs after the cross in each of the three paths are indicative of the fact that the believer must take up the cross daily and continually. It is not to be construed as a one-time appropriation that results in uninterrupted victory. The anatomy of these "downers" and the way back to victory is the subject of the next chapter.

SIX
THE ANATOMY OF A DOWNER AND THE WAY BACK TO VICTORY

In the book so far, the emphasis has been placed on the path to the cross of Christ and the victory that is known through appropriation of our death and resurrection with Christ. Indeed, this is the primary purpose of the book. However, since little has been mentioned regarding the walk afterward, some may think that the cross is a one-time event with no defeat or episodes of sin afterward.

Comparatively little emphasis has been made so far regarding our regaining and maintaining victory. Surely it will be lost from time to time. It is vital, then, that the overall process of losing, regaining, and maintaining victory be discussed.

The diagrams in the last chapter show hills and valleys after the appropriation of the cross in the life of the believer. Immediately after the cross is a peak, indicating victory, followed by a valley showing defeat, a return to the self-life or a walk after the flesh. This is what we refer to as a "downer." The believer's experience at this point will be in direct correspondence to the manner in which his flesh has been programmed in his developmental years and in his previous Christian walk. Those who had some fairly severe emotional disturbances may experience regression to a measure of this. Others may be fairly well adjusted and merely experience a loss of power in their lives and witness. Still others may become ensnared again in a particular besetting sin. Usually the defeat will not be of the magnitude known before the experience of victory. But some have regressed to similar emotional, thought, and behavior patterns that typified their previous fleshly walk. It is imperative that we take into account that the flesh (self) can never be improved—even after the cross has become a reality in the life of the believer. This assertion is made that we might appreciate the absolute necessity of the daily walk in the Spirit, denying ourselves and taking up the cross daily (Luke 9:23), which is the thesis of this chapter.

THE WAY DOWN

Having agreed on the point that all of us will experience "downers," we need to look at a profile of such a downer and understand the dynamics involved. The purpose in doing this is twofold. First, such understanding is necessary if we are to recognize how to prevent their recurrence, or at least to minimize them. Second, we need to know how to deal with them once they are upon us.

In describing the progression of a downer, it might help to compare it to an airplane in flight. Airplanes have what is known as a control column, which usually has what looks like the lower part of the steering wheel of a car. The column controls the attitude of the plane, fore to aft (front to back), left to right, and altitude. It is important to keep the plane flying straight and level, but it is possible to crash while maintaining a straight and level attitude if sufficient power is not applied.

The pilot has an instrument called an altimeter which shows whether the plane is gaining or losing altitude or if it is flying at a constant altitude. If the hands of the altimeter begin to move in a counter-clockwise direction and the pilot does nothing about it, he is likely to "buy the farm down below!" But if he notices it and pulls back on the control column while applying additional power, he will regain altitude. Obviously, the sooner he detects his loss of altitude and makes a correction, the less altitude he is going to lose. But he may decide, "I want to do this all by myself." In this event, he could pull back on the control column, and the nose of the airplane will respond and point upward. However, if he applies no additional power, he will stall and fall out of the air and "buy the farm anyway!"

In this analogy, we will be using the altitude in the diagram to represent the level of spiritual victory gained by the believer. Or, to refer back to the closing pages of chapter 5, the altitude gained initially will be the peak after the cross becomes a reality. This altitude, or level of victory given by the Holy Spirit, may remain somewhat constant for a period of time and then might begin to wane. However, the believer has been seated in the heavenlies with his head in the clouds and does not have the benefit of a spiritual "altimeter" to warn him of the fact that he is about the "crash and burn." He may be so taken up with the joy of victory for the first time in his Christian experience that he is all but oblivious to the impending dangers of the world, the flesh, and the devil. As a result, he comes down to earth with a thud and sadly faces again what he had always accepted as reality. If he has not been warned that this is "par for the course," he may begin to run another pity party and have a return to fleshly living for a while. If and when this does occur, it is necessary to find victory again, just as before by being "always delivered unto death for

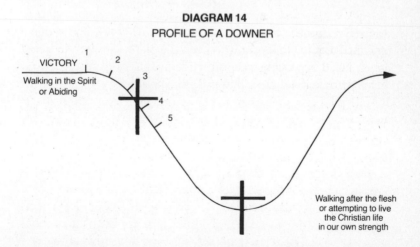

DIAGRAM 14
PROFILE OF A DOWNER

VICTORY

Walking in the Spirit
or Abiding

Walking after the flesh
or attempting to live
the Christian life
in our own strength

Jesus' sake, that the life also of Jesus might be made manifest in our mortal flesh" (2 Cor. 4:11).

First, we focus on the beginning of the "downer," since this is one of the most deceptive aspects of the overall process. The five steps at the left of the diagram indicate the progression of the "downer," the first of which may be very subtle. The more subtle the first stages, the less likely we are to have a spiritual "altimeter" sensitive enough to detect them. If not, one will lead to the other until we are back in the familiar haunts of the flesh without having the foggiest idea of how we got there.

In the gradual (or sudden) descent back to the lower regions of the flesh, I have arbitrarily taken five markers that could and should alert us that there is impending trouble. However, we can be so anesthetized by the headiness of victory that we go into a spiritual vertigo after the cross, just as some do prior to the cross. As you read the markers, which are fairly common, you may want to do some healthy introspection under the guidance of the Holy Spirit to determine what the sequence would be in your own life, such as "Pride goeth before destruction, and an haughty spirit before a fall" (Prov. 16:18). Or, in other words, the first thing might be as simple as pride. In fact, if we define pride as independence, or not abiding in Christ moment by moment, it would be the first in the sequence of failure for each of us.

For a typical example, we will make #1 as simple as negative thoughts. Once you are into this, the next, #2, might be the monster called worry. After you have worried, unhindered by the work of the Holy Spirit for a while, there could be some frustration and the decision to take matters into your own hands. When this happens, you have just hit the bottom again. That seems rather simple; but since you have always been in control of things, it is not a giant step to pick up where you left off. Also, since this may have worked fairly well for you in the past, you may be into it for a spell before you realize that your fleshly pattern of living is once more predominant.

Consider next a pattern that may not be quite so subtle but is just as difficult to discern in the beginning for those who have been addicted to this particular profile of operating in the flesh.

First, there might be a significant rejection, though it may appear trivial to the onlooker. Next might be the loss of self-esteem, resulting in #3, frustration. If the frustration is unresolved, it will result in #4, hostility. If this is internalized, there could be various degrees of depression, #5. The result is a deep crisis—another crash. Some may skip #5, depression, and crash at that point by taking it out on someone else verbally, physically, or both.

Obviously, there will be as many patterns to the reassertion of the flesh as there are people. But it may help to see that the pattern is always progressive, though the sequence may be more difficult to identify in some than in others. The point is that understanding your own particular sequence gives you a "spiritual altimeter" to enable you to assess your advance or decline in your spiritual journey. This altimeter may be "red-lined" for one or more danger points. Even if you happen to be soaring in victory and gaining spiritual altitude, there are dangers aplenty. When you are in victory, you are on the cutting edge for the Lord and have been promoted to the front lines. And, when you are on the front lines, you are very likely to get some direct attacks from the enemy of souls, the devil. Ignorance of the devices of the devil can be just as devastating as being deceived or unaware of the subtle encroachment of the flesh.

On the other hand, the emotional component in victory may be so new and intoxicating to some that the emotions may be ridden into an orbit that may be more fleshly than spiritual. Taken in this sense, an "upper" could be just as deceiving as a "downer." Since the "upper" usually does not cause as much consternation as the "downer," it is not depicted on the diagram. The point of all this is that the earlier we detect the decline, which is more general than the incline, or "upper," the less the loss of spiritual altitude.

In the beginning of the journey of learning to walk in the Spirit (Gal. 5:16), it is common for the believer to be in the midst of a downer before he is aware that he is losing spiritual altitude. It is just second nature (flesh) for the believer to revert to type and do things the way he has always done them, particularly when he is well into adulthood before he experiences victory for the first time. Often the believer may almost despair since he may think his experience with the Lord was unreal or faulty or that he can never regain victory once he has lost it. Not a few have thought that it was impossible for them ever to be defeated again, which caused them to be very disillusioned.

If this happens to find you in your first downer, or your fifteenth or fiftieth, I would challenge you to go back and retrace your steps and determine what the first event was that precipitated your downward slide. Looking back, it is very likely that it was not all that subtle. Ask the Holy Spirit to help you in determining the sequence in this particular downer, and it will possibly give you some clues to a pattern that is typical for you. Then you can use these red flags to alert you that a crash situation is imminent unless you take corrective action.

As in the analogy, it is necessary to lay hold of the control column, the cross, and apply power—the Holy Spirit's power—if you are to regain spiritual attitude. Obviously, the earlier you do this the less altitude you will lose. If we deal with the spiritual decline at its inception, *we* will know it; if we deal with it at the bottom, *everyone* may know it. It is not absolutely necessary to hit the bottom every time. But, whether you crash or pay heed to your spiritual altimeter and deal with it in its early stages, the answer is the same. However, many of us want to lay hold of the control column in our own strength and mechanically (intellectually) go through the procedure. If we do, we will find that the flesh does not cause us to regain altitude. Rather, just the opposite occurs. We fail and fall again. It is only in the power of the Holy Spirit that we will find victory, and it is in the power of the Holy Spirit that we regain and maintain a victorious walk: "This I say then, walk in the Spirit, and ye shall not fulfill the lust of the flesh" (Gal. 5:16).

THE WAY UP

To illustrate the dynamics of deliverance from a downer, we return to the diagram from chapter 2 to see two truths about redemption—the cross and the blood of Christ. In one sense, the two cannot be separated, since both occurred simultaneously, and both are vital to the finished work of Calvary. However, the Bible ascribes some of our blessings to the cross and others to the blood.

From my experience, it seems that the blood deals with what we *do* while the cross deals with what we *are*. While this seems to be true, I realize that I haven't given enough emphasis to the work of the blood of Christ in my life and ministry. This thought occurred to me as I was reading the verse:

> Of how much sorer punishment, suppose ye, shall he be thought worthy, who hath trodden under foot the Son of God, and hath counted the blood of the covenant, wherewith he was sanctified, an unholy thing, and hath done despite unto the Spirit of grace? (Heb. 10:29)

After that I began a study of Hebrews, especially chapters 8 through 10. Though my study isn't finished, some truths have emerged that have helped me understand how we maintain victory and find a way up from our downers.

You will note in the line diagram on page 110 that there is an important addition; the segment to the right joins us in our walk here below to our Lord in whom we are seated in the heavenlies (Eph. 2:6). We must understand the benefits of being seated in him before we are to walk in victory and be able to stand against the wiles of the enemy.

Since our walk in the Spirit is a moment by moment appropriation of the power of the Holy Spirit, or denying of ourselves and taking up the cross daily (Luke 9:23), and we are sanctified by the blood (Heb. 10:29), it is vital that we see the flow of power to and through us, if we are to maintain our victory in him. This continuous flow is depicted by the direction of the arrow heads in the figure 8 on its side in the diagram. As you can see, the cross, the blood, and the Spirit of God are all indispensable agents in the life of the Lord Jesus Christ being lived out through us.

The tabernacle God instructed Moses to build had three parts:

DIAGRAM 15

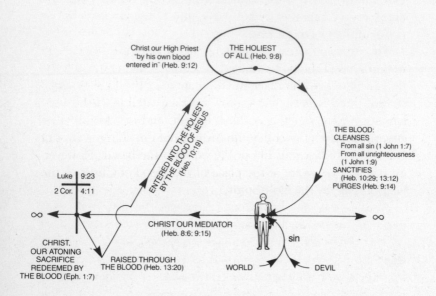

Christ our High Priest "by his own blood entered in" (Heb. 9:12)

THE HOLIEST OF ALL (Heb. 9:8)

ENTERED INTO THE HOLIEST BY THE BLOOD OF JESUS (Heb. 10:19)

THE BLOOD:
CLEANSES
From all sin (1 John 1:7)
From all unrighteousness (1 John 1:9)
SANCTIFIES
(Heb. 10:29; 13:12)
PURGES (Heb. 9:14)

Luke | 9:23
2 Cor. | 4:11

CHRIST OUR MEDIATOR
(Heb. 8:6; 9:15)

CHRIST, OUR ATONING SACRIFICE REDEEMED BY THE BLOOD (Eph. 1:7)

RAISED THROUGH THE BLOOD (Heb. 13:20)

sin

WORLD

DEVIL

the outer court, the holy place, and the holy of holies. The blood was prominent in all three of these places. Many Christians remain outer court Christians, who know that the blood has dealt with the penalty or guilt of sin. Others enter into the holy place and become involved in their worship and service and see the blood as the basis of the forgiveness of sins. Then there are those who have denied themselves and taken up their crosses and have entered into fellowship in the holy of holies, trusting in the blood to overcome the power of sin in their lives. Though all these works of God on our behalf were accomplished simultaneously for our redemption at Calvary, each must be applied separately in our ongoing walk.

It is much easier for our finite minds to grasp the function of the historical blood of Christ poured out at Calvary for our sins than it is to understand the work of his blood in our lives today in "purging our conscience from dead works" (Heb. 9:14) and "sprinkling our hearts from an evil conscience" (Heb. 10:22). Perhaps this is the reason we hear less teaching on the latter and are not more consistently buoyed up out of our downers by the power of the blood of Christ.

The verses shown at certain junctures of the Line Diagram are important and should be studied as you move along through the flow of power in the diagram. In chapter 2, the Line Diagram showed the believer's position in Christ as seated in the heavenlies, victorious over the world, the flesh, and the devil. As we enter into the reality of that vital truth, not only has the cross of Christ been efficacious in our life but also the blood. However, we may not be aware of the place of the blood of Christ in the victory given by the Holy Spirit.

At the cross, the Lord Jesus Christ was the sacrificial Lamb whose blood was shed for all mankind. The price for the guilt of sin had been paid and redemption was complete. He could say, then, on the cross, "It is finished." In heaven, he is our High Priest or minister of the new sanctuary where he has done all that is necessary to cover our sins. In us here on earth, he is our life (Col. 3:3) and our mediator (Heb. 8:6; 9:15). As our mediator, he undertakes to assure that we will keep our end of the bargain, so to speak. Therefore, we may be just as certain that he will do his work in our heart as we are that he has already done the work in heaven.

As believers, we have appropriated the truth that the blood of the Lord Jesus was shed for our sins: "And that he was buried, and that he rose again the third day according to the scriptures" (1 Cor. 15:4). However, we may not be as familiar with the truth, "Now the God of peace, that brought again from the dead our Lord Jesus, that great shepherd of the sheep, through the blood of the everlasting covenant, make you perfect in every good work" (Heb. 13:20-21). It was through the blood that he was raised to new life.

Then it was "by his own blood he entered in once into the holy place, having obtained eternal redemption for us" (Heb. 9:12). It is, likewise, our birthright "to enter into the holiest by the blood of Jesus" (Heb. 10:19). However, our "entering into the holiest" is contingent upon our flesh having been dealt with by the cross of Christ. "Having therefore, brethren, boldness to enter into the holiest by the blood of Jesus, by a new and living way, which he hath consecrated for us, through the veil, that is to say, his flesh" (Heb. 10:19-20). His physical flesh had to be rent for him "to enter into the holiest," and our veil, which is the flesh or self, prevents us from entering into intimate fellowship with him. Though the veil was rent from top to bottom in the temple, and the way for unhindered and unbroken fellowship with him was made possible, we yet have a veil of our own making, the flesh, which must continuously be dealt with by the cross and the blood of Christ. Once the Holy Spirit has illuminated the truth of our death and resurrection with Christ and it is experiential reality, we must continue to "deny ourselves and take up our cross daily."

Then, as we "enter into the holiest by the blood of Jesus" (Heb. 10:19), and by faith appropriate the truth that we are seated in the heavenlies (Eph. 2:6), we can also appropriate the work of the blood of Christ in our lives here on earth. It is necessary that we deal continuously with the defilement of sin. By confession, we are acknowledging our need for the continuous cleansing power of the blood in our lives moment by moment. As we confess our sins (1 John 1:9), and "walk in the light, as he is in the light, we have fellowship one with another, and the blood of Jesus Christ his Son cleanseth us from all sin" (1 John 1:7). However, it is easier to understand that we are forgiven on the basis of the shed blood of Christ than it is to understand how we are, within ourselves, cleansed from all sin and from all unrighteousness.

But the work of the blood of Christ in our lives goes on beyond cleansing us from what we have done. We are sanctified through his blood (Heb. 10:29; 13:12). We have "hearts sprinkled from an evil conscience" (Heb. 10:22), and our consciences may be purged from dead works (Heb. 9:14) that we may serve the living God. It is the cross of Christ that deals with what we are (or, better, were). But it is the blood that deals with what we do, and what causes us to do it—the power of indwelling sin. It is impossible to ascribe too much power to the blood, even though our finite minds will never lay hold of all that is available through the blood of Christ as the Holy Spirit ministers it to our point of greatest need.

As you will note in the diagram, the arrowheads show a continuous flow of power. In fact, you might imagine the arrows as continually moving around the "figure 8" pattern in the direction they are pointing. As we move along through life here on Earth, it is a continuous process of denying ourselves, taking up the cross daily, taking our place by faith in the heavenlies, confessing known sin, being cleansed from all unrighteousness, and having our conscience purged from dead works. Taken together, these constitute the life known as abiding or fellowship or walking in the Spirit.

If we fail to "yield ourselves to God, as those that are alive from the dead, and our members as instruments of righteousness unto God," we will do the converse and "yield our members as instruments of unrighteousness unto sin" (Rom. 6:13). Or, to put it another way, we either yield to the working of the blood in our lives or we yield to the power of sin. As we have seen, it is the Spirit, working through the blood of Christ, that is our source of continuous victory. The diagram depicts this option—yielding to the power of sin or to the power of the blood—as applied to our lives by the Holy Spirit.

If we yield to sin, we walk according to the flesh, and the power of the blood of Christ is circumvented or short-circuited. It is not that the blood is no longer efficacious but that we have failed to count or reckon upon it. We may yield in ignorance to sin's deception and walk according to the flesh while trying desperately to serve God. If so, we are in a downer and may not even know it. Once we are alerted to our plight by our own unique "spiritual altimeter," we must deal not only with *sins* but also with *sin.* We must confess the sins, but we must also deal with sin by reckoning ourselves dead to it (Rom. 6:11; Luke 9:23; 2 Cor. 4:11) and by opening ourselves by faith to the cleansing, sanctifying, purging, sprinkling of the blood of Christ. As we do, we find the Holy Spirit restoring us to the place of victory over the world, the flesh, and the devil. To put it back into the parlance we have been using, we have regained our "spiritual altitude" where we are again abiding in our risen Lord.

As we, by faith, abide in the finished work of the cross and the present work of the Spirit and the blood of Christ, it is our birthright to "produce much fruit" (John 15:5). Downers will come and downers will go, but the blood never loses its power to cleanse and restore that all glory may go to God for what he has done.

SEVEN
COUNSELING
AT THE
CENTURY'S END

There is very little substantive difference in the approach to counseling taken by some evangelicals today from that of the early seventies. Christian approaches to counseling have proliferated, with some very well trained and dedicated men and women in the forefront of the movement. Many books have been published and seminars held, but the common denominator of those who have gained prominence in the development of counseling approaches and have written about them is that they omit the message of the cross of Christ in their teachings. (If you have read the previous chapters, you will understand that by "the cross" I refer to the experience of the believer's death and resurrection with Christ, as spoken of in Romans 6 and elsewhere in the New Testament.)

This does not mean that Christian counselors who do not emphasize this truth do not have God's hand of blessing on their work. However, it is my prayer that God will encourage those who are leaders in the field of counseling to take that final step of teaching the cross.

The message of the cross, with its emphasis on death to the power of sin is not a popular message today. Yet, I believe that the experienced cross is the only scriptural way to victory because it is only the cross of Christ, and all that it means, that can deal with the flesh in the life of the believer. Anything short of this results in the strengthening of the flesh, which is a deterrent to solid spiritual growth.

Having said that, it will be apparent to the reader that Spirituotherapy has more in common with ministries characterized by teaching the cross than with those in the fields of Christian psychology and counseling. Though the message is not new, the introduction of it as a systematic counseling approach is. Down through the centuries, believers such as Madame Guyon, Hudson Taylor, Jessie Penn-Lewis, Hannah Whitall Smith, George Mueller, Andrew Murray, Watchman Nee, and a host of others have taught along the same lines.

As one might surmise, there has been misunderstanding and some misrepresentation of my counseling and theological position over the years. Without resorting to name-calling, I would like to correct some impressions you may have received, if you have read widely in the field or have attended many seminars. One prominent writer stated in one of his books that I teach the annihilation of the personality. The same writer, it was reported to me, held one of my books aloft and declared, "This is a very dangerous book!"

Some have incorrectly inferred and have stated that I teach sinless perfection. Another writer has stated publicly and in writing that I teach, or would not deny, that the believer atones for his own sin. (After being confronted on this, he softened it in a later edition of the same book.)

Another recent writer erroneously holds it to be my position that rejection is the reason we must go to the cross. Others have made erroneous assumptions about what we do, or fail to do, in counseling, and state them as facts without ever discussing them with me or a GFI representative. (Some of this is deserved, since I have not written about those things that are common to all good counseling but, rather, have concentrated on those aspects that are unique.)

Because of a faulty understanding of "exchanged life theology," some have said that we teach or foster passivity. Other things have been reported to me that have been said in various public gatherings, but I believe I have covered those that might unnecessarily weaken the confidence of the uninformed about my counseling approach. It is for this reason that I have pointed out these allegations rather than attempting to defend the Lord's work. Almost twenty years of ministry and God's hand of blessing in countless lives in this and other countries attest to its validity.

While not all Christians in the field of psychology would opt for some type of psychotherapy, certainly most of them do, despite the poor results of such treatment. Typically, many of the troublesome symptoms of the mind and emotions are mistakenly diagnosed as "mental illness," and those so afflicted begin the rounds of psychologists and psychiatrists in another vain attempt to meet their needs, either without God or as an "add-on" to their Christian faith. Since "everyone is doing it," mental health has become as acceptable as motherhood, although much less understood.

As the problem of mental health becomes an enigma that everyone recognizes and many talk about, there is a frenzy of activity, enormous outlays of money, but little permanent results. One young man to whom we ministered had been in a mental health facility for two years in addition to other treatment. His father's insurance company had paid out a reported $250,000 with little, if any, permanent change in his life. He was seen by a GFI counselor for three days, and the Holy Spirit did a major work in his life. The young man said that he knew more about himself and the cause of his problem in the first interview than he had in all of his previous treatment.

The "revolving door" syndrome or recidivism is a given in mental health, and such mental health professionals must continuously deal with it. Despite their use of many types of psychotherapy, there is little statistical evidence to support the validity of psychotherapy as a treatment modality. An article by Hans J. Eynsenck appeared in a book entitled *Sources of Gain in Counseling and Psychotherapy* edited by Bernard G. Berenson and Robert

R. Carkhuff. The article, entitled "The Inefficacy of Therapeutic Processes with Adults," read in part:

> In general, certain conclusions are possible from these data. They fail to prove that psychotherapy, Freudian or otherwise, facilitates the recovery of neurotic patients. They show that roughly two-thirds of a group of neurotic patients will recover or improve to a marked extent within about two years of the onset of their illness, whether they are treated by means of psychotherapy or not.

Despite the mounting evidence to the contrary and frank questioning within the ranks of psychotherapists as to the efficacy of their work, their offices are filled with those seeking bread but who are being handed stones, in my opinion.

It is not popular, as I have learned over the years, to challenge traditional psychiatry and psychotherapy with the view that spiritual transformation is the only solution that gives permanent change—not an adjunct, complement, or supplement. It is ironic that even some ministers are sometimes less receptive to consider such a claim than psychotherapists.

Personally, I do not think it coincidental that Freud and Lenin were contemporaries, since both were guided by the god of this world, Satan. Lenin's work provided the foundation for the political, economic, and social revolutions that we have witnessed in this century. Freud's work completed the unholy alliance by bringing into being a counterfeit approach to dealing with soul troubles that has, in my opinion, played a major role in undermining the morality of millions around the world.

Few have made the connection between Freud's pronouncements about the centrality of sexuality and the "free sex" of the sixties and seventies and the "safe sex" of the eighties and nineties. Still fewer have discerned the undermining of the spiritual fabric of our country, to say nothing of our churches, by his godless influence and by the common acceptance of humanistic approaches to psychology. He is the acknowledged grandfather of modern psychology and liberalism has ridden into many seminaries on the back of psychology. Many have maintained a thoroughly orthodox theological position while espousing approaches in the psychology classes about the immaterial makeup of man that are antithetical to that being taught in the theology classes.

At the same time, I believe there are many Christian psychotherapists who are sound in their faith and fundamental in doctrine. They do much to alleviate the suffering of emotionally disturbed people, returning many of them to a fuller life. But sometimes the apparent success is deceptive. Good psychological adjustment in a Christian is many times mistaken for spiritual maturity and alleviation of symptoms is frequently termed a cure. The person may be active in Christian work, even in the ministry, and yet be out of adjustment spiritually. Psychotherapy helps a person to meet his own needs, to learn more effective ways of thinking, feeling, and behaving, and to develop more adequate defense mechanisms. What the person may be missing is the truth Christ spoke, "Without me ye can do nothing" (John 15:5). As self (or *ego*, as Freud would define it) grows stronger, there is an increase in pride and a decrease in humility and dependence upon God.

Psychotherapy has as its goal a stronger person. But God's goal for us seems to be dependence upon himself. As Paul wrote, "When I am weak, then am I strong" (2 Cor. 12:10). Anything that teaches us self-reliance, then, is at cross purposes with the Holy Spirit and a substitute for his work in our lives.

It is one thing to help a person understand the dynamics of his thoughts, emotions, and behavior, but it is entirely another thing to use psychological principles exclusively to attempt psychological and behavioral change. The underlying presupposition, if the psychological and functioning and behavior is more acceptable, is that the person will feel better and will be changed in the process. In other words, to change the thinking and behavior is to change the person. To some degree this is true or therapists would no longer be in business. God, however, works on another principle of change—transformation—to change

119

the person so that the behavior can change. God works through the conversion experience and through the transformation that occurs when we enter into union with Christ.

Spirituotherapy does not use the term "mental illness" since by definition it would suggest that the problem is in the mind. While structural or organic anomalies do exist, such as brain tumors, brain abnormalities, or defective biochemistry, these, being organic rather than functional, are not generally considered to be "mental illness."

There is, for example, sound research showing that a chemical imbalance exists in the brain in severely depressed patients. For this reason, at Grace Fellowship International, we try to work with medical professionals when we deal with such depression. But it has not been proven to my knowledge, however, which comes first—the depression or the chemical imbalance. Since we have seen many patients come out of clinical depressions literally overnight, the chemical imbalance—if it did exist in these patients—obviously gave way to the work of the Holy Spirit in these cases.

Some who are highly respected in the field of mental health are also rejecting some of the notions of "mental illness." Among these are William Glasser, M.D., Thomas S. Szasz, M.D., and Dr. Garth Wood. Szasz stated in the preface of his book, *The Myth of Mental Illness* (Harper and Row), "Although mental illness might have been a useful concept in the nineteenth century, today it is scientifically worthless and socially harmful."

In a more recent book (1983) entitled *The Myth of Neurosis* (U.S. edition by Harper & Row, 1986), Dr. Garth Wood accepts the fact of psychiatric illness but gives the lie to much thinking, feeling, and behavior that has been commonly accepted as the domain of psychotherapy. His book begins:

> In this book I have sought to expose the conspiracy to extend indefinitely the boundaries of mental illness. For far too long people have been led to believe that the person suffering from an excess of life's problems needs "expert" medical and psychotherapeutic intervention, thus allowing the "patient" to qualify for

"illness," to the ultimate detriment of his mental equilibrium and often at considerable financial cost. Such a view is dangerous nonsense. If we are not ill then we are well, although we may be unhappy.

Although Dr. Wood does not offer spiritual answers to the dilemma he presents, his "Moral Therapy" is more tenable from a human standpoint than much of that which is marketed today under the guise of "mental illness." On the cover flap of his book is the statement:

> Neurosis is a myth. Its bogus status as an illness has stigmatized millions of perfectly normal people whose chief deficiency is their inadequate approach to problems and their unrealistic expectations of what life should bring them. By encouraging the damaging "illness excuse," therapists promote the illusion that patients are not responsible for their predicament and, therefore, are powerless to help themselves.

Wood further states, "I define psychiatric illness so that it [neurosis] can be excluded. What remains is individuals who are responsible for their predicament, slaves to neither their environment nor their brain biochemistry, and who are therefore free, with support, to change themselves for the better."

In his book *Reality Therapy* (Harper & Row, 1975), Dr. William Glasser also rejects the concept of mental illness. His basic tenet is that bizarre behavior is merely an ineffective attempt at meeting one's needs, and that a person must meet his needs through another person. In his words:

> At all times in our lives we must have at least one other person who cares about us and whom we care for ourselves. If we do not have this essential person, we will not be able to fulfill our basic needs. One characteristic is essential in the other person: he must be in touch with reality himself and able to fulfill his own needs in the world.

There seems to be a contradiction here, however. How would one find a person who is able to fulfill his own needs if everyone has to have some other person to do this?

This, too, is the basic premise of Spirituotherapy. The prime difference is that the Person who meets our needs is the Lord Jesus Christ—not a human therapist. If Glasser's book were read with this significant substitution, the approach of Spirituotherapy would be approximated. While denying that mental aberrations constitute mental illness, both Glasser and Szasz would endorse a type of human therapy.

Though the problem is ultimately spiritual in nature, the obvious manifestation is through psychological and behavioral symptoms. In his book *The Crisis in Psychiatry and Religion* (D. Van Nostrand Co., 1961), Dr. O. Hobart Mowrer takes a strong stand in favor of a spiritual emphasis in meeting the needs of those who are in emotional and mental distress. He wrote:

> If religious leaders had been deeply involved in the care and redemption of seriously disturbed persons for the past century, instead of systematically "referring" such persons, there would have been no Freud and no necessity for a Tillich or a Fosdick to try and legitimize him.

Even though the symptoms are mental and emotional and some benefit relative to communication is derived from classification of such symptoms, to attempt therapy in the realm of the psyche or mind is folly since it is merely symptomatic treatment. Some symptoms respond in varying degrees to psychotherapy, although the source of the problem is seldom, if ever, touched in the process. In Spirituotherapy, there is no benefit in differential diagnosis from a psychological standpoint. This is merely a taxonomy for symptoms. Since the source of the problem is ultimately spiritual in nature, it is infinitely more important to determine the spiritual state of the individual. The person rarely cares which particular psychological phenomenon has been his plight, so long as he discovers how to unload it. Some people coming to Grace Fellowship International have been labeled during previous visits to psychotherapists. Some were given little hope for recovery, and others were told outright that they would never be any better. However, God did not honor such prophecy.

We have seen God deliver many people from various symptomatic ailments that now pass for mental illness or emotional disturbance. Some of the more common ones are depression, anorexia nervosa, bulimia, homosexuality (given the honored status of an alternate life-style by psychiatry in 1973), obsessive-compulsive behavior, obsessive thoughts, behavioral problems, addictions, and most other types of so-called neurotic disturbances. Also, many have been set free who have had psychotic episodes. It seems that some of those who have been diagnosed and treated for paranoid schizophrenia have definite organicity and will have to be continuously treated with medication unless God chooses to do a physical healing as well. We have not found chronic schizophrenics to be good candidates for spiritual counseling in an outpatient setting.

The counselor in Spirituotherapy is not a therapist but a spiritual guide. The therapy is accomplished by the Master Therapist, the Holy Spirit. His work within the human spirit results in deliverance from psychological symptoms caused by spiritual maladjustment. This is not to say that all psychological difficulties have a spiritual genesis. Many, if not most, of these stem from early childhood, as we discussed earlier in Chapter 1, or from some significant trauma. Psychology is beneficial in understanding some of the behavior that follows, but the use of psychology in treatment is often counterproductive. For the person who is unwilling to have God's answers, or is unaware of God's answers, psychotherapy is his only recourse for symptomatic relief. But it is not the answer for the problem.

God did not promise to meet our emotional and mental needs through a counselor, psychologist, or psychiatrist just as he did not promise to meet our visceral or physiological needs through a physician. He did say, "But my God shall supply all your needs according to his riches in glory by Christ Jesus" (Phil. 4:19). Spirituotherapy takes Paul's position literally, unequivocally, and unapologetically, and trusts God to honor his Word and perform a miraculous deliverance in the life of each person who comes for counseling.

If the counselor is to be able to tell a person with any conviction that God will supply all his needs, then the counselor must provide the example by casting himself completely upon the Lord even in the matter of salary. The commitment of the counselor must pervade every area of his life if he is to be a guide and example to those with whom he shares Christ. This is in direct contrast to that of conventional psychotherapy. In many forms of therapy, the therapist is not required to have experienced what he prescribes. And, in some approaches to therapy, the therapist is not encouraged to be congruent in the relationship but to maintain the professional facade of the therapist-client relationship. Records are replete with cases where the therapist is unable to meet his own needs in the world. Statistics show that for many years the suicide rate for psychiatrists has been the highest of any profession—mute evidence to the failure of the therapeutic climate to meet the deepest needs of people—clients or therapists.

God's purpose in redemption was not just to forgive us of our sins and help us live with our problems by harnessing our flesh to "work for him." Christ came not just to reconcile us to himself, but to save us from ourselves by his life (Rom. 5:10). He came to give us life more abundantly (John 10:10). It is estimated that 90 percent of all Christians never experience the abundant or victorious life, so they do not understand how deep psychological problems can be resolved by letting the Lord Jesus Christ manifest his life in them, instead of resorting to human therapy. This same is true of many pastors, Christian psychologists, and psychiatrists. Though Christian in their orientation to life, they resort to therapy as a means of showing people how needs can be met.

Even in Christian educational institutions, it has become commonly accepted to relegate the treatment of mental and emotional disturbances to the "professionals," which means that many believers are referred outside the church for the solution to problems of the soul that only the Holy Spirit working through yielded believers could resolve. Thus, the turf is neatly carved out to the satisfaction of both disciplines. The behavioral sciences are more than happy to have this lucrative referral source and those trained in theology do not have to deal with sticky situations of behavior. In fact, many escape the acid test of the efficacy of their particular theological positions by ascribing to another discipline the responsibility for treating those in soul trouble.

A MODEL OF THE FIELD OF COUNSELING

The chart on the next page might aid the reader in comparing and contrasting what is done in the arena of counseling. Although the behavioral sciences could be more thoroughly covered by addressing the fields of psychology and psychiatry, this chart restricts itself to the arena of counseling. It is assumed that counselors do not handle to the same depth problems usually treated in psychotherapy, but the line of demarcation between psychotherapy and counseling is often blurred.

In the chart, the secular module is inclusive of psychiatry, psychotherapy, and counseling so far as the presuppositions are concerned. The four major forces listed are Psychoanalytic (Freud), Behavior Modification (Skinner, Watson), Phenomenological (Rogers), and Transpersonal (Edgar Casey, et al). There have been numerous offshoots of each of these, with just a few being shown in the chart. The fourth force, Transpersonal, or the occult in its various forms, is the most rapidly proliferating at the present time. Naturally, the cross in all its dimensions is *decried* by therapy that is based on godless presuppositions.

The Christian approaches to counseling have been divided into those that are more psychological and those that are primarily theological. The psychological approaches are rooted in the secular approaches with the exception of the Transpersonal, which is largely based on the occult and Eastern religions. Though those in Christian psychology would utilize Scripture and scriptural principles in varying degrees, some type of psychotherapy is taking place since that is the work of the psychologist whose work is consistent with his training and title. As such, the cross is *denied* as having the power to release suffering people from

125

DIAGRAM 16

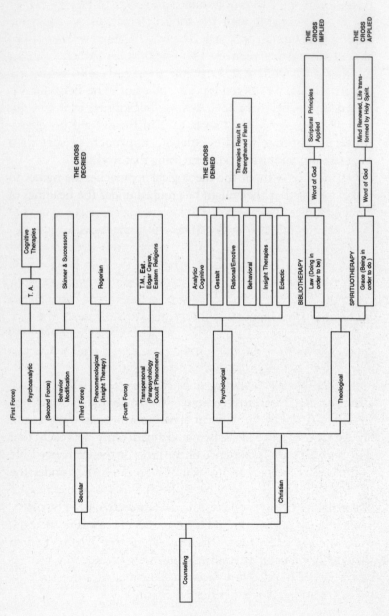

126

mental and emotional disturbances without therapy.

The analytical/cognitive approaches trace their origins to Freud, even though some would deny much of Freud's theory. These deal primarily with the thought processes, as the name implies. The Gestalt approach is heavily freighted with emotional content and was pioneered by Fritz Pearles. Albert Ellis put together the cognitive and the emotional and called his variety of psychotherapy Rational Emotive Therapy. The Behavioral is rooted in the Behavior Modification of Skinner, while the insight therapies trace their roots to Carl Rogers and his client-centered approach. The Eclectic approach is sort of a smorgasbord, taking a little of anything that works.

Distinctions without the theological approaches are harder to make, except that they might be grouped under the headings of Law and Grace. Approaches that look to the experienced cross of Christ as the method and goal are under the heading of grace, while the category of Law would apply to those that major on self-effort with the Lord's help. Those in the Law group would teach that one must *do* in order to *be*, while those in the grace category would teach that we must *be* in order to *do*. Though the Word of God is foundational to both, in the case of the Law approaches, scriptural principles are applied by counselor and counselee without the cross having become a reality. Change may take place in the life, but *exchange* has not.

It is possible for counseling to be Bible-centered without being Christ-centered or cross-centered. Christ-centered counseling (grace) will always be biblical, but biblical counseling is not always Christ-centered as herein defined. Any approach that does not make the experience of the cross or the exchanged life central to its method and goal might be categorized under the heading of Bibliotherapy, while those that inculcate the message of the life in Christ are here called Spirituotherapy. The chart, while not exhaustive, might help the reader in assessing methods of counseling and remove the mask from that which, though thoroughly biblical, strengthens the flesh because the cross is *implied* rather than *applied*. From my position, these are the only two alternatives; it is either flesh or Spirit.

127

If I understand the Bible correctly, the abundant life and anxiety are mutually exclusive, as Paul wrote, "Be anxious for nothing. . . . And the peace of God which passeth all understanding shall keep your hearts and minds through Christ Jesus" (Phil. 4:6-7).

All Christians enjoy peace *with* God through redemption, but relatively few enjoy the peace *of* God. It is this peace that the neurotic or psychotic person is desperate to know. It is likewise this peace that the so-called "well adjusted" person needs, even though he usually does not understand that he has a problem until his comfortable world begins to fall apart at the seams. In either case, the discipline of adversity, faithfully administered by our sovereign Lord, is often necessary before we begin to seek him with all our hearts (Ps. 119:71; Jer. 29:13).

Abundant life or the Spirit-filled life is not God's portion for merely a chosen few. God intends that all of his children go beyond knowing Christ as Savior and Lord to know him as *life*. It is to this end that this book is dedicated. It is not written just to the professionals in the field of theology and the helping professions, but to any searching soul who sincerely wants to know the Lord Jesus Christ as "all, and in all" (Col. 3:11).